MW01716303

OUTSIDE THE BOX TO BOX

OUTSIDE THE BOX TO BOX

Experience the Joys of Connection by
Creating a Rewarding Social Life

TAK MAEDA

ROCKETSHIPPUBLISHING.COM

Copyright © 2021 by Tak Maeda

All rights reserved. No part of this book may be reproduced in any form on electronic or mechanical means, including information storage and retrieval systems, without permission in writing from the publisher, except by a reviewer who may quote brief passages in a review.

Although the author and publisher have made every effort to ensure that the information in this book was correct at press time, the author and publisher do not assume and hereby disclaim any liability to any party for any loss, damage, or disruption caused by errors or omissions, whether such errors or omissions result from negligence, accident, or any other cause.

This book is not intended as a substitute for the medical advice of physicians. The reader should regularly consult a physician in matters relating to his/her health and particularly with respect to any symptoms that may require diagnosis or medical attention.

The events in this book are true. Names and minor details have been changed for privacy and legal reasons.

This paperback edition first published in 2021

ISBN: 978-1-7775902-0-8 (paperback)
ISBN: 978-1-7775902-1-5 (e-book)

Published by Rocketship Publishing
rocketshippublishing.com

Tak Maeda is a Japanese-Canadian author. After experiencing and overcoming the struggle of the lack of social connection when working a full-time job, he set out on a mission to help those in similar positions create a rewarding social life through self-improvement. In Outside the Box to Box, he successfully communicates his ideas to readers in a way that is easy to read, understand, and implement.

If you would like Tak Maeda's help with improving your social life, please visit rocketshippublishing.com/consulting.

Contents

CHAPTER 1

The Box-to-Box Lifestyle

Tell me if this sounds familiar. You wake up on Monday morning; get ready for work; commute to work; work for eight or nine hours; commute home; spend your free time watching television; playing video games; scrolling on your phone or computer, and eating; and then you go to sleep and do it all over again five times until the weekend. Then when the weekend rolls around, it's more of the same—just without the work.

Maybe you go to the gym, run some errands, do an activity, or meet up with a friend, but those events seem to be rare occasions.

If this sounds familiar, that's because it's the life that many people in the workforce live—me included.

When I first started working full time, it became my life. Go to work, go home, go to work, go home, repeat until Friday, become happy on Friday for some reason, then spend the weekends at home alone. It wasn't uncommon for me to try to avoid telling people about my weekend on Monday morning because I always spent the time alone and never had anything good to share.

I realized I was living the box-to-box lifestyle!

I invented the term *box-to-box lifestyle* to describe when your life is spent going from one box to another. One box is your home; the other box is your workplace. Pretty much the entirety of your life happens in one of two boxes or commuting between them. If you work from home, your house serves as both boxes.

Living box to box for a day or two isn't a bad thing, but I imagine for most people reading this, that scenario isn't just a one-time thing. It pretty much describes your daily life—and your weekends aren't much different. The problem with this is the routine—of working a job, then going straight home for a technology-fueled isolation session—is that it's the perfect breeding ground for loneliness, as there is very little room for real social connection.

Loneliness Is a Problem

The problem with loneliness is that it goes completely against human nature and our happiness.

Humans are social creatures because we evolved to be. Evolution is the result of DNA's primary goal. Almost everything is in service to this core biological goal: to survive long enough to successfully reproduce.

Survival is simple: don't die before you can reproduce. Reproduction is more complex. It's one thing to reproduce your DNA, but it's another for that reproduced form to survive and reproduce again (and again and again). In order for that to happen, the individual and the partner they choose to reproduce with need to have good genes. Also, their life conditions need to be strong for them to continue passing on their genetic lineage.

Humans have survived and thrived for millions of years because they created strong social groups that worked together to achieve specific goals. We don't have extraordinary strength like lions, bears, or sharks do. We can't fly or travel fast like eagles or cheetahs can. We don't protect ourselves with poison like frogs or snakes do. But we do have extraordinarily intelligent brains and can communicate to each other in ways that other animals cannot. That's our evolutionary advantage.

Humans are social because we have to be. Being social is how we survived and thrived as a species. We used the collective abilities of each other to fulfill our evolutionary goals. We did this by forming strong social bonds and communities. Each individual human left alone would stand little chance of surviving as we are relatively weak creatures, but put us into groups, and we can use our intellectual ability to work together. After millions of years of validation, the evidence is clear: humans are better off with strong social connections.

When you are alone, you stand very little chance of accomplishing your DNA's goals of surviving and thriving. Living on your own—in the dark, cold woods, fighting off wild animals and diseases without any help—is pretty much a death sentence. Even if you already have children, being isolated from them increases their chances of dying too. That's why our DNA has been hardwired to avoid loneliness and, by extension, rejection—as rejection was and is usually the cause of being ostracized from the group.

If all this seems a little primal and irrelevant, that's normal. But you must understand that even though society has changed dramatically, and modern times have stripped away a lot of our survival conditions (and made the world quite a safe and habitable place for us), our instincts are still hardwired in us. Evolution takes hundreds of thousands of years to change, not decades.

It's important to understand our instincts and how they served and continue to serve us. Happiness and fulfillment come from satisfying the requirements that we were evolutionarily designed to satisfy. Here are some of our basic instincts that guide our behavior that you may subconsciously understand but haven't yet logically connected.

- **Evolutionary social instincts:** It's the reason why you feel good when you do something nice for someone. It benefits everyone to help the people you care about.
- **Evolutionary dietary instincts:** It's the reason why eating healthy foods make you feel good. Healthy foods give you the nutrients required to survive.
- **Evolutionary sexual instincts:** It's the reason why getting cheated on is such a horrific experience. A man unknowingly raising another man's offspring, or a woman's partner's attention being diverted to another woman is a recipe for reproductive disaster.

This Is What Loneliness Actually Is

According to many experts, loneliness isn't necessarily about being alone or isolated. Instead, it's about *feeling* alone or isolated. Although being physically alone and isolated often leads to this feeling, loneliness is not just limited to those who are on their own.

Celebrities, who are often the complete opposite of being physically alone, who often have their significant other and entourage around them, and who are often chased by their screaming fans and chaotic reporters, can feel very lonely. College students who are constantly around people in their dorms or in classes can feel lonely. Even members of a loving family who all live under the same roof can feel lonely.

The feeling of being alone or isolated doesn't come from not being surrounded by people. Instead, it comes from a lack of connection. When you don't feel connected to another person, yourself, an idea, a task or an activity, or the world, the feeling of loneliness creeps in.

You may be slightly relieved to know that more than three out of five Americans are lonely, with more people reporting feeling like they are left out, poorly understood, and lacking companionship, according to Cigna, an American worldwide health services organization. This number has been rising significantly and all indicators point to the continuation of the alarming trend. This is not just limited to the United States. Many developed countries are experiencing a similar trend, according to Statistics Canada and the Jo Cox Commission on Loneliness in the United Kingdom.

Knowing this data probably doesn't make you feel that much better, but realize your loneliness is definitely not a problem that's exclusive to you. You're not alone in feeling alone; we're all going through it together.

Circumstances Change

Since the industrial revolution, humans have started doing something that is historically unprecedented for our species. We've survived and evolved by creating social tribes and communities, but more recently—especially since the 1950s—we've started to go in the opposite direction. More and more people are opting to live away from home and on their own.

While there are many benefits that come from living on one's own, the trend of people living on their own has undoubtedly contributed to the loneliness crisis, since more people are choosing to be isolated from the social networks that we've depended on for millions of years.

But it's not just that. There is something more subtle yet impactful going on.

On April 30, 1993, the web became public domain. What the creators of the internet may or may not have known was that their creation was going to alter human history forever—for great benefit and for great pain.

Before the internet rose to dominate society, humans had to be quite social in order to function. Back then, in order to do things, we needed human interaction. Now, not so much.

Instead of calling a store and placing an order for a product, we can hit a button for same-day shipping. Instead of dealing with an actual business front operator, we can click around on a website. Instead of retaining office space for employees to work amongst each other, more and more companies are choosing to operate remotely. Instead of picking up the phone and talking to a friend or meeting up with them in person, we can send them a text or a social-media message instead.

On social media, we sometimes don't even communicate in the English language. We send our friends or family funny photos or videos, and that becomes our version of communication.

When we as a society live in isolation and have less social interaction, we get exactly what you'd expect: a loneliness crisis.

The subtle reason why people are becoming lonelier and more socially isolated is both the effect and the cause of our new environment. People don't get a chance to develop their social abilities to a point where those abilities can help serve their needs in the world. People are becoming more socially anxious and avoidant; we take longer to build real conversation skills (if we do at all), and the ability to be intimate is becoming rare.

Happiness Is in Social Relationships

One of the world's longest studies of adult life, done by Harvard, found that high-quality social relationships are the strongest link to lifelong happiness, even over money or fame. Social ties protect people from life's discontents, help to delay mental and physical decline, and are better predictors of long and happy lives than social class, IQ, or even genes.

At the end of the day, the only things that will bring true meaning to your life are your relationships with other people, whether they be close connections or relationships with acquaintances, community, and yourself. Pretty much everything you do in your life is in service to your relationships. Our modern technology, status, money, perfect photo moment obsessed culture tends to lose sight of this at times.

I think this is something we all know instinctively but haven't yet logically connected. Looking back, some of the happiest moments of my life weren't because of fancy meals, luxury events, or vacations, but because I was with someone that I cared about. My happiest moments growing up were sitting in a McDonald's or in the dining room of a superstore with my best friend; on a patio outside a mall in Japan drinking juice with my brother; or on a drive with great friends singing along to music.

If you ask an elderly person about their biggest regret, you will most likely find that it has to do with their relationships with the people they care about. It's almost never about work or money.

When we understand that social relationships are tied to happiness, we can see why social relationships remain among the top priorities for people, up until their dying breath. We can also see how unfulfilled social relationships end up as people's biggest regret.

Let me be among the first to come up with a complete guide that covers all the aspects of social relationships and solves the problem of how to maintain them and thrive within them—not just throw a collection of unrelated "tips and tricks" at you, like you'd see in an internet article or online video.

My ultimate goal in writing this book is for you not to wait until you're eighty years old and on a hospital bed to realize that social relationships are the most important part of life. Instead of looking at our actions and behaviors in hindsight, I want us to look at them with foresight, so that we have the chance to enjoy life, while we have lots of it left for us.

The next chapter will show you how to set effective goals that take into consideration your life situations and needs. This chapter will help clarify how to find the maximum enjoyment within your social life.

Chapter 3 is going to outline how you can create strong connections with people you like. For some people, reading this chapter and the next will be all you need. If that solves your problem, amazing—thanks for reading!

But a lot of people will need help developing the skills and traits that will allow them to form and maintain strong relationships. The rest of the book, from Chapter 4 onwards, is dedicated to just that.

Chapter 4 shows you how to effectively meet new people, which is the building block of forming relationships.

Chapter 5 is about the key skill you need to develop in order to be successful socially: vulnerability. I define *vulnerability* as being willing to express your true desires by putting yourself in uncertain situations. Almost everything you need to do to be successful socially—whether it's talking to a new person, asking them to meet up, or strengthening a relationship—requires vulnerability.

Chapter 6 shows you how to optimize your body to get the energy, confidence, and cognitive sharpness you need to make your social life flourish.

Chapter 7 helps you learn to feel comfortable and positive about yourself in social situations. Feeling comfortable and positive are the two feelings that people must have to enjoy a social interaction, because those two feelings are required to feel safe.

Chapter 8 teaches you social skills. The practice of communication is important to creating strong connections with others. Connection is an emotional process, and effective communication will help you to arrive at authentic connection.

The last chapter, Chapter 9, is about enjoying the time you spend alone. Regardless of how good your social life is, chances are you're going to spend a fair amount of time alone.

You may learn a lot of new concepts from this book, or this book might feel basic and confirm what you already know. The information in this book is made to be simple. You must understand that the point of this book isn't to intellectually stimulate you, but to solve the problem you came here to solve. It's not just enough to know what to do; the whole point of this book is for you to actually do it in your own life. Straightforward information is the quickest path to action and success.

Although this book may feel like a process, the goal is very simple: to get you to a point where you are capable of developing strong connections with people you choose.

That goal may seem like light-years away, or it may require only a few adjustments. Either way, this book will walk you through the steps. You might need to come back to this book or to a specific chapter many times, but that's the idea. Then maybe one day, you'll set this book down for the last time, as you'll feel like you no longer need its support. The goal of this book is to help you get to that point, but it's up to you to put in the thought and the effort. The journey is more than worthwhile—it is, perhaps, the most worthwhile journey of your life.

Key Takeaways

- It's not uncommon to live the box-to-box lifestyle, where your life happens exclusively in one of two boxes: your house or your workplace.
- The box-to-box lifestyle tends to lead to loneliness, since there is little room for social connection.
- Loneliness is a problem because it goes completely against human nature and our happiness. Humans are hardwired to have strong social connections, as this is what helped us survive and thrive as a species.
- Loneliness is when you *feel* alone or isolated.
- More than three out of five Americans feel lonely, with other developed countries experiencing similar trends.
- The leading causes of loneliness include more people living on their own and technology reducing our need to be social.
- The strongest link to lifelong happiness is the strength of our social relationships.

CHAPTER 2

Social-Life Goals

If you look at the trophy, you'll miss the target. If you look at the target, you'll get the trophy.

It's extremely important to identify the problem we face and to dream of possible solutions. But in order for you to succeed at adapting the outside-the-box-to-box model into your life, you need to identify the target you want to hit. It's only then that you'll receive the trophy.

You can identify your target by setting goals. More specifically, identify what it is that you actually want out of your social life. Creating a rewarding social life isn't a one-size-fits-all solution, as different people have different needs and circumstances. However, goals can be distilled down to a few different types. Before we get into the different goals, you must become aware of what you need from your social life and what social styles best suit you. This will help you to focus your effort on the goal that will bring you the most happiness and satisfaction.

What Are Your Needs?

Relationships are about fulfilling the needs of the people in them. Although we typically understand this part, we sometimes forget that our needs have to be fulfilled as well.

As you read about the following needs, keep in mind that your needs don't necessarily have to fit neatly within this list. Your needs can be a combination of the needs listed here, or they can be separate needs altogether.

With that being said, feeling like you need any one of the following is totally normal and okay. You are a human, and humans have needs. We're identifying them now, so you know what you need to get from your social life.

FUN

Is your life missing fun and excitement with friends? If you feel like your days are spent working and coming home to an uneventful evening, you may be missing entertaining dinners, hangouts, parties, trips, and memories with your friends.

COMPANY

If you find yourself spending the majority of your time alone or feeling alone, you may need the constant company of people to keep you from isolation all the time.

EMOTIONAL SUPPORT

Do you have little to no friends or family you can turn to in times of crisis or sadness? Without people to support you when you need it, you may feel that you have no safe place to land, which can cause you to be anxious or stressed.

INTIMACY

Perhaps you know a lot of people without knowing many people *well.* And perhaps a lot of people know you without knowing *you* well. Knowing someone intimately can bring you a level of connection and friendship that wouldn't be possible with acquaintances or casual friends.

Are You Introverted or Extroverted?

Although a good portion of people are usually both introverted *and* extroverted, if you lean more toward one side or another, you may have a distinct style of being social.

Generally speaking, introverts prefer to spend more time alone. When they do spend time with others, it's with small groups of closer friends. Extroverts prefer to spend more time with others and with larger groups of people, even if they aren't necessarily close friends.

But these identities are not fixed. Chances are, you have both introverted and extroverted tendencies. The purpose of identifying whether you lean more toward one side or another is to find out the social styles you best respond to.

If you're unsure of whether you're more introverted or extroverted, just listen to your instinct. Would you rather go to a big party or have a small dinner gathering with close friends? Do you tend to dominate group conversations, or do you typically stay quiet in the background, only talking when you have something relevant to say? Do you feel more energetic and excited when you're with a big group of people or when you're with someone you really like and care about?

What Are Your Priorities?

Assuming you voluntarily picked up this book, it's fair to say that the creation of your social life is going to be a high priority. I highly doubt that anyone, if they're being honest with themselves, is reading this book and thinking of the creation of their social lives as a low priority.

The question is: How high is the priority? Though the majority of readers might name their social lives as a high priority, it may not be their *highest* priority. What you choose to prioritize will greatly determine how you create your social life.

If your social life is your top priority, it means that your social life is more important to you than your career, hobbies, or other interests—which is totally valid. If you identify your social life as your top priority, making decisions in your social life will be much easier, since your attention and effort can be focused on that single goal. Your main concern is to make sure the other aspects of your life remain functional, while you pursue your top priority.

If your social life is a high priority but not quite at the top of the list, that is completely valid too. Perhaps a more important thing consumes more of your attention such as your career, a task you're currently working on, a hobby, or other interests. If you identify that your social life is your second priority, you may need to divert your attention and effort mostly into your first priority. You'll become free to focus on your social life once your attention and effort is off of your main priority.

If your social life is a medium priority, as in you have two or more things you prioritize over it, or you need to devote all your time to one thing, this is definitely valid, too. Perhaps a combination of your career, family, hobbies, and other interests take precedence over your social life. Creating your social life at this point can become tricky, since it's not going to be nearly as important as what you do on a daily basis, and your social life may suffer as a result. It's definitely possible to create a social life you love, but managing it may pose a challenge.

How Often Do You Want to Be Social?

All social lives are different. Some people prefer to live on their own and see their friends when they choose, while some people prefer to be constantly surrounded by others.

Setting a Social Goal

Broadly speaking, social goals can be categorized into four different types. These types are by no means mutually exclusive; if you feel like you want to create a combination of the following, by all means, do so. It's important to know that *you* choose which social goal(s) to pursue. You can also choose to change your social goals at any time. These are not permanent declarations of how you're going to live for the rest of your life. If you have different needs at different times, feel free to adjust your goals as you see fit.

CLOSE FRIENDSHIPS

Developing close friendships with select people is a goal you can set for yourself. Having close friendships means that you have people in your life who truly love and care about you, know the details of your personal life, and whom you are willing to be open and emotionally vulnerable with.

The benefit of having close friendships is that you have people in your life that treasure you—this is something you must cherish if you are lucky enough to have it. You also have a level of intimacy with them, which allows you to share your personal life. These are going to be the people with whom you share the special moments of your life.

Although close friends have far more benefits than drawbacks, one potential drawback is that they can hurt you, whether they intend to or not. Also, if you just focus on close friends without having a wider social network, you may still feel disconnected from people who aren't your close friends.

Everybody deserves to develop close friendships. If you're new to creating your social life, developing at least one close friendship could be your first goal, as this will be the most beneficial to your life.

NUMBER OF FRIENDS IN YOUR NETWORK

Having a large number of friends and an expansive social network is another goal you can set for yourself. This would mean that a lot of people know you, like you, and are social with you.

The benefit of having a large network is that you'll have many people to be social with. You'll also have lots of life opportunities, as many people within your network can open doors for you. And, you'll have a sense of belonging to a wider community of people.

The drawbacks of having a large number of friends and an expansive social network is that it can be difficult to manage at times, and it can open you up to more sources of drama and problems. Having an expansive social network without having *close* friends can leave you feeling lonely, as you may lack the depth of intimacy.

Nonetheless, a wide-ranging social network is great for extroverted people, people who need more fun in their lives, people who want more company, and people who are looking to be social very often.

GROUP OF FRIENDS

Having a group of friends is another goal you can set. The benefit of having a group of friends is that you have a tribe of people you belong to, which is an invaluable feeling. These people can bring you the fun, excitement, support, and intimacy that close friends can bring to you individually. But within a group, there's strength in numbers.

The drawbacks of having a group of friends include conflict in the group and difficulty branching out to other social groups. Managing a group of friends can also be time-consuming.

Having a group of friends can be a great option for both introverts and extroverts. The group shouldn't be so big that it makes introverts feel uncomfortable, but it shouldn't be so small that it makes extroverts feel restricted. Depending on the group, these friends can help fulfill many of your needs, including fun, company, emotional support, and intimacy.

LIVING SITUATION

Improving your living situation is another goal you can have. You could have an amazing social life outside of the house, but if your living situation causes problems, it can result in overall dissatisfaction with your social life. Whether it's because you live alone, the people you live with aren't making you happy, or where you live isn't making you content, it's worth improving if you feel like you need to.

Improving your living situation can dramatically improve your day-to-day life. Maybe you move in with better roommates or with a romantic partner, improve family relationships; move to another part of the city, another city, or even another country; or live in a better home.

The drawbacks of trying to improve your living situation is that it can be expensive, tedious, and scary. However, improving your living situation for the better versus tolerating a comfortable but unsatisfying experience will almost always be a good decision.

ROMANTIC RELATIONSHIPS

Getting into a romantic relationship with someone you like can bring intimacy and sexual connection into your life. Although we are not going to go into too much detail in this book about finding a romantic partner, the good news is that treating dating as an extension of your social life will make the process much more fun, less stressful, and more successful. Romantic relationships and other social relationships share one crucial thing in common: human connection.

By improving your ability to connect with humans in general, you will improve your ability to connect with someone you want to be romantically involved with.

A romantic relationship can provide a number of amazing benefits and experiences that other social relationships may not, namely intimacy, romantic connection, and sex.

The drawback of a romantic relationship is that the potential emotional complications will likely be the most intense out of all the different types of relationships in your life. If you focus only on your romantic relationship, your social life will most likely suffer. This could cause you to become more dependent on your romantic partner to fill in the gaps—which can cause even more problems.

A romantic relationship is a great goal for people who are looking for new meaningful experiences that prove enriching.

Key Takeaways

- Creating your ideal social life isn't a one-size-fits-all solution. People have different desires, so it's important to set the appropriate goal(s).
- What are your social-life needs? What would you like your social life to give you that it currently doesn't? Is it fun, company, emotional support, and/or intimacy?
- Depending on whether you are more of an introvert or an extrovert, the style of your social life may differ.
- Being clear with yourself on how often you want to be a social will help determine what goal you set.
- Goals for your social life can include close friendships, a large number of friends and an expansive social network, an intimate group of friends, a better living situation, and romantic relationships.

CHAPTER 3

Outside the Box to Box

"Congratulations, you just became CEO." Imagine if you finally got the biggest promotion of your life. You're beaming with excitement, so much that you run out of the office into your dream car, a Rolls-Royce, and speed home. After you arrive at your luxury home in the rich area of town, you make your way inside and do a happy dance, open the bottle of Dom Pérignon you've been saving for this day, and order the nicest steak dinner you can buy. Overflowing with excitement, you grab your phone to call your best friend and tell them the great news . . . but you've forgotten that you don't actually have any true friends. A little bummed out but still hyped up from the news, you run upstairs to tell your spouse and hope for some celebratory play . . . but you realize that you don't have a spouse you love, or any children, for that matter. Your family doesn't live in the same city, so you can't make your way over to their houses. The big empty house that you find yourself in is starting to seem like a symbol for your life.

That story illustrates how the box-to-box problem can be a big issue, even if you finally manage to achieve your goals—in your career and financial status—and gain material possessions. At the end of the day (or life), your feelings about yourself after you've achieved everything you thought you wanted truly depends on the strength of your connections to people around you. Are these people there to celebrate you? What if you got the worst news of your life? Would they be there to support you?

The solution to the lack of connection and loneliness that results from living the box-to-box lifestyle is to strengthen your connections to the people you like and to spend as much face-to-face time with them as possible. Doing this will bring you a consistent source of human connection from those you love and trust, and who care about you in return.

The goal is quality over quantity. Having a small group of close friends with whom you are connected will make you feel far more fulfilled than having a large network of casual acquaintances or having hundreds of social-media followers, although all have their benefits.

The solution consists of two parts. First, you must have strong connections with those who you truly like. The benefits of having social relationships—the joy, the emotional fulfillment, the support system—all come from strong emotional connections, not shallow, casual connections. Second, you need to spend as much face-to-face time with your friends as possible. Even if you have strong connections with close friends, if you don't see them consistently, you may still feel quite lonely. Texts, social-media posts, and video calls don't create the same emotional fulfillment as having your friends physically in front of you.

Keep in mind that when I use the word *friends* here, I am referring to anyone you have a strong social connection to. This can include coworkers, romantic partners, family members, or anyone you know.

Intention Builds Friendship

The key to creating a social life you love is being intentional. Be intentional with the people you choose to strengthen connections with, and be intentional about strengthening those connections. Creating a social life is not a passive process—you must intentionally create the moments along the way.

PICK WHO YOU ACTUALLY LIKE

Although you may know on a subconscious level whether or not you like someone, it's good to be conscious of why you do. People you like are typically going to be people you have fun being around, people you respect, people with a similar level of intelligence and social ability as you, people with similar interests, people you trust, people with similar values, and people with similar life goals.

Building friendships requires an investment of time, and you want to choose your investments wisely. A study published in the *Journal of Social and Personal Relationships* found that, on average, it takes fifty hours of time with someone before you consider them a casual friend, ninety hours before you become good friends, and over two hundred hours before you become close friends.

In the adult world where everyone is busy with work and life, fifty, ninety, two hundred hours are meaningful amounts of time that you just won't get to have with everybody. The older we get, the more we realize that our biggest asset isn't our money, houses, or cars, but our time. When we were little kids, spending two hundred hours with someone could happen within months, but as adults, our time is much more limited. Use your time wisely; spend it with people you actually like.

There is a lot of truth to the saying, "You become the sum of the five people you spend the most time with." You start adopting the personalities, mindsets, behaviors, and habits of those around you. When you're going about picking the people you want to be better friends with, ask yourself, "Would I be happy if I became more like them?" This should clarify who you actually want to be friends with.

STRENGTHEN RELATIONSHIPS WITH THOSE YOU LIKE

So, you've intentionally found a person or people that you like—great! But the intention doesn't stop there. It's on you to take an active role in developing the relationship. The other person may like you quite a bit, but they might also be nervous or shy, or they might have a richer and busier social life than you. In short, they may be caught up in other things. This is common and normal, but you should take the initiative, nevertheless. This is your life, remember?

Contact Is Crucial

The logic to building friendships with other people is indisputable: to be closer with someone, you have to spend more time with them. Although in-person time is going to serve as the bedrock of your friendship, texts, calls, and internet-based communication can be supplemental. People are busy with their careers and lives, yourself probably included.

We can be quick to bash smartphones nowadays; however, they're undoubtedly powerful tools to help us keep in touch with those we would've otherwise lost touch with. A new friendship would likely fall apart if it wasn't for social media, text messaging, video chatting, or talking on the phone.

Keep in mind that friendships aren't always formed linearly. They don't always unfold in the order of meeting, hanging out, casual friendship, and strong friendship. Some of your closest relationships may be with people you've known for years but never spent a lot of time with. Your closest relationships could also have many starts and stops along the way.

Priorities, Priorities, Priorities

There is an opportunity cost to developing a friendship. Like anything that requires both your time and effort, there comes the cost of not using that time and effort on other things. Although it's entirely possible to have a great career, exciting hobbies, fulfilling friendships, a partner you love, and a family, there are also things to which you must not allocate your precious time and effort to if you want to keep your social life among your top priorities.

What you typically have to sacrifice is the micro-level stuff. This includes spending money frivolously, watching TV, playing video games, scrolling on social media, engaging in trivial hobbies, and so on. These activities are fine, but they do take away the time, energy, and resources you could be using on your relationships. They have their time and place, and by no means am I advising you to get rid of them completely, but you may find yourself leaving the TV turned off for a night and choosing to meet up with a friend instead.

If you're doing this for the right reasons and with the right people, it shouldn't feel like a sacrifice at all. It should feel like a trade in which you're getting a bargain, because you are.

The head of my department at a startup where I worked tried to get me to understand this, but I think I was a little too naive at the time. I've always been a pretty frugal guy out of necessity. I moved to a new city, away from family, for university, so I've had to support myself. When I had internships, I saved all my money, so I could survive the school semester without working a part-time job. So yes, I was pretty frugal with my money.

The department head tried to explain to me that it's worth investing in relationships with people you care about, whether that be going out to get drinks, food, or attending an event with them. In the end, prioritizing a relationship over the little bit of savings is going to be more beneficial. Does that mean spend recklessly? Absolutely not, and I don't think that will ever be the case for me, given my personality and lifestyle. But it took me a while to truly understand what he meant.

This concept applies to anything you choose to prioritize. Chances are, if you're struggling with your social life, there is something you're choosing to prioritize over it, consciously or not. For people like me, it's money. You figure that it's more cost-efficient to eat at home than to invite a friend out to meet you for dinner. For some people, it's video games or television. The next three episodes of *Game of Thrones* or a night with your *League of Legends* team might sound way better than spending time at a social event. For some people, it's work. Finishing the project you're working on feels more important than taking the evening off and meeting up with a friend. For some people, it's nothing external. Not being vulnerable and exposing yourself to rejection feels more comfortable than taking the initiative to text a friend and get together.

At the end of the day, it's about your priorities. What are you choosing to prioritize?

Be Proactive

Being proactive in your relationships means showing up for your friends. Show up physically for your friends by hanging out with them and attending their events. Show up emotionally for your friends by being there for them during tough times, helping them in ways that are meaningful, celebrating their wins, and keeping yourself up to date with the things going on in their lives.

Physically showing up for your friends means actively creating social activities for them to join. Instead of asking them if they want to hang out, suggest a time and place, then ask them if they want to join you. Being proactive means taking the initiative instead of leaving the burden of responsibility on them.

Showing up physically for someone is just as important as showing up emotionally. A friendship is more about being connected emotionally than just occupying the same physical space for extended periods of time.

Showing up emotionally for someone means being an active part of their personal life. Check in, and remember the important moments in their life such as dates or events, accomplishments, job interviews, and family occasions. When they are going through something personal, ask them about it. It can be lonely and frustrating when you've just gone through something significant, whether it be good or bad, and no one is there to validate or support you during it. If you're a good friend, that someone is you. As a friend, you want to see *your* friends do well in their personal life too. This is where you make an effort to help them succeed in whatever they are doing.

Your friends are human, and they will inevitably have their own struggles, whether those struggles be centered around work, personal life, health, dating, family, or other relationships. The same concept applies: show up for your friends, and be proactive in reaching out to them or helping them.

When offering help, stop saying, "Let me know if I can do anything for you," or "I'm here for you." Unfortunately, these platitudes don't mean much, and they place the burden of responsibility on the other person.

As a proactive friend, you can say: "I'm here for you. Can I do ___ for you?" If you can't think of anything to offer, you can try, "I want to help you, but I'm not exactly sure what I can do. What is the best way I can support you right now?" These questions show that you are taking on the responsibility of helping, which is far more thoughtful than forcing someone to be vulnerable when you were the one who wanted to help.

Dating Disaster

My friend "Kenji" was texting back and forth with a woman he was interested in. I was checking in and staying updated throughout the process. Suddenly the woman, "Emily," asked him to hang out. Kenji was ecstatic!

Kenji and Emily texted until the day before the date. Kenji updated me on what was going on. He mentioned that Emily didn't seem too excited about meeting with him, even though Emily was the one who asked Kenji out. Naturally, I was a little confused, so I asked Kenji to tell me about what he had planned for the date.

Kenji told me that he asked Emily to go on a walk along a trail like last time (they met up once before). In my perspective, it didn't take much to realize why Emily wasn't thrilled about seeing him, because all Kenji did was ask her on a walk again. I immediately told Kenji that he needed to plan something more special than that. Dogs get excited about going on walks, not women. Sometimes, things that sound obvious aren't so obvious, but I didn't judge him because I would've made a mistake like that a few years ago. He was starting to think his chances were slipping away, but I told him there was a solution. He was relieved and thanked me for being there. Hold on, buddy, we still have lots of work to do!

All Emily was expecting was a boring trail walk. I told him that he could make the date more special by planning a small picnic after—getting take-out food when the walk ends. He thought this was a great idea, so I told him to find a take-out restaurant that they would both enjoy. I instructed him on how to find a good place and let him do his research. I also told him that he needed to take the lead on the date instead of asking for her input all the time and expecting her to initiate, which is what Kenji usually resorts to.

He got back to me a few hours later with an idea about where to get food. He settled on bar food, and I told him it was a solid plan. He asked me what else he needed to prepare for the date. The only thing left was his clothes. I asked him what he was going to wear, and he told me he was going to wear black joggers, a T-shirt, and sneakers. I told him that it wasn't a bad casual outfit, but he was missing something big. He was confused and asked what he was missing. I told him if she was the one to ask him out, that meant she liked him, which also meant she was probably going to dress up nice for the date.

Kenji's mind was blown! He realized that yes, Emily was dressed pretty nicely when they met up the first time. With that in mind, we settled on a slightly upgraded version of his original outfit (he's not much of a dress-up kind of guy) and left it at that. Kenji also asked me to meet up with him two hours before their date, so we could talk and get him in the right state of mind. I agreed. It was getting late in the night at this point, so we decided to talk the next day.

That was where everything went downhill. Since the date was at 7:00 p.m., we decided to meet at 5:00 p.m. He called me in advance to tell me he was going to be a bit late. Not the best start to his date, but at least he was late with me and not with Emily.

We exchanged a couple of text messages. Then, he hit me with these texts.

> Kenji, 5:10 p.m.: "I might need you to take my bag if that's alright."
> Kenji, 5:11 p.m.: "It kinda looks invasive if I have a big sports bag."

I was completely dumbfounded. Why did he have a big sports bag? Did this guy not realize he was going on a date? I was half laughing but half in complete shock from the sheer stupidity. I didn't want to carry a big sports bag on the walk home, either, but I didn't want to jump to any conclusions, so I asked him why he had a sports bag.

> Kenji, 5:13 p.m.: "That's a good question. I always bring around a sports bag."

Have you ever had one of those moments where you genuinely can't understand what someone was thinking when they made a decision? This was one of those moments for me.

It gets a lot worse.

> Kenji, 5:31 p.m.: "Also should I ask her now where we should meet or leave it till the last minute?"

HOLD UP! YOU DIDN'T CONFIRM THE DATE???

Remember when I said the only thing that was left for him to do was prepare his clothes? It didn't even occur to me that doing something as basic as confirming early in the day was something he'd miss, but I was wrong.

Keep in mind that this was at 5:31 p.m., an hour and a half before the date, and Emily had no idea if the date was happening or not, because Kenji didn't confirm.

As soon as he told me he hadn't yet confirmed, I knew the date wasn't happening, although I didn't tell him that. I was hoping Emily would ignore this boneheaded move because she liked him, but I knew that was unlikely.

As predicted, Kenji told me that Emily bailed on the date. He proceeded to question what this woman was thinking. I was pretty annoyed because he still didn't understand. But since I'm his friend, I explained exactly what he did wrong and how he could improve. I didn't pull any punches during the explanation. I told him to meet up with me anyway, so that we could talk more.

We met up as planned, and I asked him how he was doing. He was in a surprisingly good mood—whether or not it was just a mask to hide his pain, I didn't know. When we talked about Emily, he laughed, not taking the situation seriously. At that point, I started to get heated. I asked him why he was so giddy and said that if he wasn't going to take this seriously, I would walk away and let him suffer in dating forever. He immediately snapped back to reality and apologized, so I explained exactly what he did wrong.

We ended up talking for a good hour. By talking, I mean me explaining everything and Kenji being confused, shocked, and angry at himself.

Basically, all of his problems stemmed from the fact that all of his dating experiences have been with women who came to him. He hadn't put any thought or effort into his dating life. I told him that unless he's rich, famous, extremely good looking, or has an amazing lifestyle, women won't be doing that too often. And the women that he wants to date most likely won't. This is true for most men, me included.

He told me that he felt so bad for not realizing this. He was furious with himself for making these mistakes. I told him this was a learning experience and he probably wouldn't ever make the same mistakes again. I recommended he read a good dating-advice book. By *recommended,* I mean I pretty much forced him to read it, but he recognized the value, so convincing him wasn't that hard. I said to him, only half-jokingly, "If I have to smack you over the head with this book, so the contents bleed into your brain, I will, but I'd rather you read the book."

We laughed pretty hard about it, but I think he understood my seriousness.

Kenji is a pretty solid guy. I have no doubt he's going to find himself someone he really likes and who really likes him. Hopefully, he doesn't make as many stupid mistakes as he did with Emily.

The point of this story is that I used my gifts of experience and knowledge to help out a good friend. This was only possible because I was proactive enough to keep myself updated on his life. When the subject of his date came up, he was in a great position to receive the help that he desperately needed.

Drill this concept into your head: *be proactive in your social relationships.*

Be Thoughtful

Being proactive in your relationships can also mean being thoughtful. Being thoughtful means you do things to benefit the other person for the sake of the friendship, without being asked to.

Unless you're naturally thoughtful, you can help yourself to become more thoughtful by asking, "If I were my friend, what would I appreciate right now?" There are basic, everyday things that everyone would likely appreciate, like bringing a friend a cup of coffee, buying them lunch, giving them praise and compliments, or asking them to spend time with you—but where your effort becomes impactful is when you tailor it to a specific person. Doing so requires you to have some sort of previous connection and knowledge of that person's preferences.

This is a made-up list of imaginary people's preferences, but take it as inspiration:

- Bring them tacos because they were craving tacos
- Bring them sushi because they got stood up for a sushi date
- Recommend to them your favorite dating-advice book because you two talked about dating struggles
- Send their resume to someone in your network who may know about a job opening for them
- Prepare meals for them because they're sick in the hospital but still need to take care of their kids
- Offer help planning their anniversary date with their partner
- Insist you do a mock job interview together when you know they have a big job interview coming up
- Get them a small gift to pay respects for a loved one that passed away recently

What to Do Together

By now, you should understand that you need to spend lots of time with someone to develop a strong relationship with them. The question now is: What do you do together?

Regardless of what you do, the main factor that will drive your friendships is the quality of your conversations, since conversation leads to connection. However, *what* you do while having those conversations can play a big role in supplementing your connections.

Eating Food / Having Drinks

The most culturally accepted way to hang out with someone is to get food or drinks with them. This is one of the most comfortable ways to bond with someone, since everybody is used to the idea of going to a restaurant or bar.

Play

Playing together is an underrated way to build a friendship. When you and your friend are playing, you are focused on having fun and enjoying yourselves, and in doing so, supercharge your connection.

Play is not something that only kids do; it's something that adults forget to do. We get so tied up in our jobs, finances, responsibilities, relationships, and being "mature" (whatever that means), that we forget we can have fun. Screw having boring coffee meetups—go kick some soccer balls!

Playing removes a lot of the pressures that come with socializing, such as trying to impress each other. It's hard not to have fun when you're running after a Frisbee at full speed or playing a close game of *FIFA*.

That's the idea of play. Pretend you and your friend are little kids again, running around, having fun, and not caring about anything else other than enjoying yourselves. Little kids don't care about how impressive they are or how foolish they look. They aren't preoccupied with their phones (or at least our generation wasn't); it's just free-flowing fun and emotions.

Here is a small collection of play ideas:

- Sports
  - Basketball, soccer, tennis, football, Frisbee, bowling, golf, martial arts, baseball, hockey, volleyball, archery, kayaking, rock climbing, skateboarding, skiing, snowboarding, swimming, shooting
- Games
  - Billiards, darts, card games, poker, board games, paintball, laser tag, mini golf, escape rooms, arcade, video games, virtual reality, amusement park
- Art
  - Painting, drawing, creating music, freestyle rapping, dancing, cooking, baking, making films
- Exploring / adventuring
  - Hiking, visiting a new place, travelling, trying new restaurants

Achieving the Same Goal

Sometimes, friendships can develop as the result of two people attempting to accomplish the same goal. This works best when the goal is one that takes time to develop—this means you and your friend will have many hours' worth of bonding as you try to accomplish your goal.

I once ran into a guy I knew from school during my last year of university studies. I had a class with him previously, and he seemed like a cool guy. I always saw him around campus, but I never hung out with him, so when we saw each other this time, we made plans to get drinks.

A week or so later, we met up. We immediately clicked as we started talking—it was like we were friends who had known each other for years. We talked about business, school, work, health, podcasts, and women. It became evident that we were both interested in improving our dating lives, so I asked him if he would like to work together on our current situations. He was curious since, no one had ever asked him that before but he said sure.

Just like that, I was able to spend a few hours every week hanging out with a cool, genuine guy and attempting to accomplish a goal I wanted to achieve. We're still good friends irrespective of our dating lives, but working together to improve our individual situations with women made our friendship much stronger.

Any goal you and someone else have in common can be the basis of a new friendship. Depending on the goal, you can meet up to directly accomplish it, or to talk to and support each other in your individual quests.

Common goals can include:

- Relationships
- Dating
- Family
- Raising kids
- Career
- Promotions
- Getting a job
- Career development
- Making more money

- Building a business
- Self-improvement
- Health
- Fitness
- Social life
- Spirituality

Hang Out

If the quality of your interaction is good enough, you don't necessarily need to do anything special to have a good time and develop the friendship further. Some of my best moments with my friends have come from just walking around and talking with them, because the quality of the conversation was so wonderful.

Whether it's walking around, sitting somewhere, or going over to a friend's house or having them come over to yours, hanging out is a comfortable, inexpensive way to spend time with someone.

Consistency

As we know from the *Journal of Social and Personal Relationships* study, it takes many hours to build a friendship, and we are quite busy people. You and your friend will need to communicate and spend time together consistently, so you can get in those quality hours. You don't need to create a schedule for your meetups (though you can if you want), but you do need to make an effort to reach out on a regular basis.

Strong friendships aren't developed from one-off events or moments, but are built by small, consistent actions repeated over a long period of time. This is reality, not Hollywood.

Groups

All of the information in this chapter also applies to groups. You don't need to be in a one-on-one situation to build friendships—you can do it in groups, as well. In fact, groups are preferable, especially when you're first starting out, because groups help you create a tribe of people to whom you belong. The support and companionship that a good-quality group can bring is priceless.

If you're looking to create a group of friends from scratch, you need to either host a gathering with a collection of people you like, or build individual relationships with people and introduce them to each other with the goal that, over time, you'll all hang out together.

Trust

Trust is the biggest factor in any relationship. Trust is something that you either have with someone or you don't. Sure, it exists on a spectrum, as there are certain things you can trust people with and not others. You may trust a person to be a kind person, but you may not trust them with your deepest insecurity. But, if you don't have a strong perception of trust in another person, it will be almost impossible to build a true friendship with them.

The ingredients of a good friendship include emotional connection and time. Strengthening a connection with anyone requires trust. If there's no trust, there's no hope for authentic connection.

Building trust is not as straightforward as not lying or not sharing secrets, although not doing either of these things is huge. If you don't live your life with honesty, integrity, and vulnerability, you're setting yourself up for people to distrust you. If you aren't a reliable person to yourself, you are most certainly going to manifest this quality in your relationships, intentionally or not. Being honest and living with integrity is the absolute nonnegotiable minimum for a strong relationship, but there's more.

Your Word Is Your Bond

Do you live up to your word? When you say you're going to do something, do you do it? While you may be quick to say yes, think about it for a moment. While not living up to your word isn't necessarily lying, it's not being honest either.

Not living up to your word can affect the trust another person has for you. This happens when someone begins to view your word—your primary form of communication—as inaccurate and unreliable. If someone is emotionally invested in your word and then you betray it, you'll likely exacerbate the distrust that person has for you. If someone plans an event and you said you were going to attend but don't, you affect the reliability of your word—doubly so, if you don't give sufficient notice. If you say you're going to do someone a favor and you don't follow through with it, you affect your credibility.

Wasting Time

Do you waste people's time?

This one doesn't exactly sound like it's related to trust, but it certainly is. When someone makes an effort and allocates time to meet up with you, they are doing so on the premise that you are a good, interesting person. If you betray that expectation and waste their time—what diminishes are their expectations and, by extension, their trust in you.

You can waste people's time in a number of different ways: being late, being selfish, talking about yourself too much, being boring, being negative, complaining, whining, arguing, creating problems, criticizing or being socially uncalibrated.

Keeping Your Mouth Shut

Do you keep secrets?

If you're being vulnerable with another person and that person is being vulnerable with you, it means they trust you enough to share things that are personal and sensitive. What do you do when you hear these things? Do you run around to people you know and tell them, or do you keep the information between you and the person who confided in you? There are few things that feel more betraying in a friendship than realizing that the person you trusted shared something that was meant to be private. Talk about a friendship killer.

Mental Security

Do you let your insecurities get the best of you?

At first, mental security doesn't seem to bear a strong relationship to trust, but it most certainly does. Remember, trust isn't just about not lying—it's about being honest and having integrity. Letting your insecurities get the best of you compromises your integrity. Your insecurities can get the best of you in a number of ways. You may react poorly to other people's success, criticize yourself and others too much, or sacrifice your identity too often in order to please others.

It's important to know that everyone has insecurities. Even the people who you think are perfect have their own insecurities. Of course, some people may have deeper insecurities than others, but to think that someone has no insecurities just means you don't know them well enough. If a friend makes you feel insecure, you don't have to be around them. This may not be their fault, nor yours—it's possible that what you're experiencing is a mismatch of emotional states. This is normal—simply work on overcoming your own.

Do you find yourself becoming overly jealous or bitter towards other people's success? It's normal to wish you were in someone else's shoes, but the reality is that if you socialize with people, you will come across a large number of people who have it better than you do, or have it better in certain areas of their lives, whether those areas be career, finances, lifestyle, appearance, romantic relationships, family, social ability, talents, and so on.

If another person makes you insecure, you don't have to fake being happy or unbothered, but if you start lashing out, overcompensating, getting competitive, or making attempts to tear people down, the other person will quickly pick up on your behavior, and their trust in your character will likely deteriorate.

Do you complain or criticize too much? Once again, overly complaining or criticizing is a sign of underlying issues that you haven't worked through yet. These issues manifest through anger.

Do you find yourself supplicating to others? Supplicating to others means you defer power, respect, and authority to someone you perceive as better than you. It's normal to be in a friendship dynamic where one person is perceived to be better (however you choose to define that), but how does the "lesser" person react? Do they take inspiration and continue to have a horizontal relationship, or do they supplicate and create a vertical relationship?

The difference between a horizontal and vertical relationship is that in a vertical one, there is a clear power and authority difference, while in a horizontal relationship, both parties see each other as equals. Unless the person who is on top of the vertical relationship is a narcissistic jerk who tries to hold power over the other, chances are the vertical relationship is present because the lower person is acting in ways that create such a dynamic. This can be done through sucking up to the other person through excessive praise and compliments, fearing the other person, holding back, trying too hard not to make the other person have a negative response, being overly nervous around them, etc. I've been on both sides throughout my life, and I can attest to the fact that my being on the lower end of the vertical was entirely due to my actions and thoughts. The same goes for when I was on the top of a vertical relationship. I'm not a narcissistic tyrant (or at least I don't think I am), and I don't do much to make other people feel lesser, but whether it was because of how I carried myself, how "successful" I was in my life at the time, or my ability to be social, the other person in the relationship supplicated.

Although you may like feeling powerful, understand that feeling powerful is hollow and fleeting. It's an ego trip, but it doesn't do any good for forming a friendship, since the mismatch in integrity or respect is sure to cause problems—even if both of you are honest, well-intentioned people.

Best Friends (Not) Forever

Not all people are going to become your friends, and not all of your friends are going to be your friends forever. This isn't necessarily a reflection of you as a person (although it can be). The bigger point is the importance of finding those who you are compatible with, which is not going to be everyone.

WHEN TO BREAK OFF A FRIENDSHIP

The obvious reason to break off a friendship is when you don't like the other person. You don't need to justify to someone else (or yourself) why you don't like them, but if you don't want to have that conversation, it's best for everyone if you stop pursuing the friendship. You don't need to justify your feelings.

By the same token, if someone doesn't like you, stop pursuing a friendship with them. The other person doesn't have to justify why they don't like you. If you intentionally put in effort and that person doesn't reciprocate after a reasonable period of time, this may be a sign to break it off.

Another big reason why you might want to break off or stop pursuing a friendship is if you don't share the same values. You two could like each other quite a bit, but your differences in values could inspire you to invest your time and effort elsewhere. You're going to inevitably become similar to those you spend lots of time with, and you may realize that while you might like someone, you aren't willing to adopt their values or lifestyles.

Consciously understanding differences in values might make others think you're shallow, rude, or picky, but that's simply not the case. Values are values for a reason—because you find them to be important. If your values are important to you, you will be critical of those who don't share the same ones. This doesn't make you a bad person, just a person with strong values.

You cannot force friendships either. People are people—they make their own decisions, and some of those decisions include not being friends with certain individuals. Don't try to force a friendship, and definitely don't sacrifice your own self-respect for one.

HOW TO BREAK OFF A RELATIONSHIP

The great thing about removing friends from your life is that there are no lawyers or children involved in the divorce, and there is no dramatic breakup that's required, unless of course you're breaking off a romantic relationship or a marriage. You simply have to stop hanging out with them. Stop inviting them to your events, stop sending them texts, and communicate your thoughts to them if need be. Your friendship(s) will slowly fade away, although you may need to directly express your issues if the other person doesn't get the message.

Key Takeaways

- The solution to the box-to-box lifestyle is to have a social life with friends with whom you have strong connections and that you see often face-to-face.
- The key to creating this social life is to be intentional. You do this by intentionally picking who you actually like, then intentionally strengthening relationships with those you like.
- It can take upward of two hundred hours before someone becomes a close friend. Choose who you spend your time with wisely.
- People you like are typically going to be people you have fun with, people you respect, people with a similar level of intelligence and social ability as you, people with similar interests, and people with similar life goals.
- To develop relationships you enjoy, try to establish consistent, face-to-face contact with your friends.
- You need to develop trust in order for a connection to grow and flourish.
- You can break off friendships when you feel it's not working, whether it's because you don't like the other person, the other person doesn't like you, or your values interfere with the friendship.

CHAPTER 4

Seven Billion People to Meet

Life is an open-world game, not a one-player simulation. When you spend the majority of your time alone—looking at screens or with earbuds in—life can easily seem like a single-player video game where all other humans are non-player characters, but real life is not like that. Every single person in the world is a real, living person who can become a part of your life journey (shocking concept, I know.)

The crazy thing is that there are more than seven billion people in the world and counting. Although you won't even come close to meeting a fraction of a fraction of them, this shows there are many people you can meet in your life, and no, they're not all background characters.

One of the skills you will most likely need to cultivate in order to develop deep connections with others is meeting new people. Unless you already have potential people with whom you can be good friends, your future friendships are going to come from people you haven't yet met.

The First Interaction

The good news is that cool people are everywhere; the problem is that you'll need to start conversations with them—which requires taking initiative and overcoming fears.

SMILE

Set a strong first impression before you even say a word. If there is one instant change that can make you ten times more successful socially, it's smiling. When you smile at strangers and they smile back at you, it immediately removes the first thing humans assess about someone else: threat level. A smile communicates that you're not a risk. It signals that you're friendly, in a good mood, or more importantly, mentally stable (at least in the moment). Fun, approachable, happy people smile. Depressed, angry people usually don't.

In order to have great interactions with people, they need to be receptive toward your personality and conversation. Once they perceive you to be nonthreatening, they lower their guard and become free to open up and be receptive toward you. A person who is unsure if someone else is a threat will likely always lean toward assuming a threat. That's why you may receive an unpleasant vibe around people who don't smile, who can't keep eye contact, who stare, or who speak too fast. Your brain is either coding them as a threat or is ambivalent, which can prompt your instinct to tell you to run! Smiling at people takes some vulnerability, but if you do it, you'll find that you can start an interaction much more easily.

When you smile at someone and that person smiles back, you can move right into, "How's it going?" You two have acknowledged each other and are now building familiarity, even if it's only been seconds since your initial interaction. In short, you both have exchanged a positive signal. Starting a conversation from that point onward should feel natural.

SAY IT WITHOUT THINKING

When you want to start a conversation with someone, but you're not yet a natural at it, chances are you're going to be quite nervous. In order to start a conversation from that state, it's best to say what you want without allowing your mind to second guess itself. When you do this for the first time, it's going to be a strange feeling, because there will be a moment when your brain doesn't realize you're already in conversation.

Similarly, if you have to walk over to talk to someone, the difficult part is actually walking over. Your brain may be against doing this due to the fear of uncertainty, but the trick is to move your feet and start walking without overthinking it. When you do this, your brain goes into conversation mode, since you're on a one-way street to that person. The good news is that starting the conversation is the most difficult part. If you can do this successfully, it only gets easier from there.

HOW TO START A CONVERSATION

Conversation starters can fall under one of three categories: a question, a comment, or a direct starter.

Questions are the safest way to start a conversation since you're not necessarily starting a conversation right away. Instead, you are creating the opportunity to start a conversation. You can ask questions about the place you're in, such as the restaurant, gym, or office, or you can ask questions about the other person, such as an article of clothing of theirs you find interesting, what they're doing, or what they're thinking about.

The thing with questions is that if you ask a neutral question that doesn't spark emotions—for example, asking for directions—and you want to create a conversation, make sure you follow it up with a question or statement that *does* spark emotion, or else you may be stuck in a boring, uneventful dialogue.

Comments are a great way to start a conversation because of the creative freedom they lend. You can make a comment about the situation you're in or about the person with whom you're speaking to. Similarly to questions, comments can be focused around the place you're in or something related to it. Comments about the person with whom you're speaking can also take the form of a compliment.

When giving a compliment, try to be specific about what it is you're complementing. Specificity can help make your comment more unique and meaningful, since you may be calling attention to something that the person with whom you're speaking has never heard before.

A direct conversation starter requires no context. Openings like "How's it going?" and "Hello" are examples of direct starters. For the longest time, I thought that I needed to come up with some elaborate, creative, relevant question or comment in order to start a conversation with a stranger. Who am I to turn to the person next to me and say hello? Well, it turns out that hello is an effective opener. Always make sure to offer a hello with a smile and a positive intention.

You Don't Need an Elaborate Reason to Talk to Anyone

If there is one thing that being social has taught me, it's that you don't need an elaborate reason to talk to someone. I used to think I needed a logical reason to start a conversation with someone, but I now realize this was merely my fear or lack of social skills talking.

I've used this principle in my personal life with friends, women, or when making small talk with whomever. It's not uncommon at all for me to start a fun conversation with a cashier, a waiter, a person sitting next to me at a restaurant, co-workers, fellow students, people in the same group situation as me, people at the gym, someone on social media, or wherever else, because I learned that I don't need an elaborate reason to talk to anyone. Granted, I still get nervous a lot of the times, but I do it anyway.

Of course, there are going to be various fears you will have to work through if you want to start talking to people you've never met before, but just know one thing: you don't need a grand, legitimate reason to talk to someone. Usually those types of rationalizations are just that—rationalizations.

The Blue-Backpack Beauty

One freezing winter evening, I'm walking home from university. I'm waiting at the crosswalk, the same crosswalk I've waited at for the last four years—but this time would be different.

There's a woman waiting a few meters in front of me. She seems cute, but it's kind of hard to tell under her winter jacket with her hood up. Did I forget to mention it's absolutely freezing where I'm at? She turns to me, we make eye contact, and she smiles. My guess is correct—she's very pretty.

I want to talk to her, but I want to start off the conversation on a strong note. I notice she has this really cool blue backpack on with a neat artsy design, so I walk over and say, "Hey, this is kinda random, but that's a really cool backpack you have on. I love the design."

She appreciates the compliment. She replies with a cheerful "Thank you," and we start talking.

One thing I sense immediately is that she has a lovely personality. We cross the street together, having a fun conversation. It's nothing out of the ordinary, but it *is* a friendly, entertaining chat. We get to the other side of the street, and talk for a minute more.

For the purposes of teaching you a lesson about not needing an elaborate reason to start a conversation with someone, the story serves no further purpose—although you may want to learn how to avoid making a big mistake I made.

In my mind, the conversation seems like it's coming to an end. I think that I should get her contact information, whether it be her cell phone number or social media handle.

Then fear kicks in. My brain rationalizes my fear by convincing myself it's not a good idea to ask for this woman's contact information because the whole conversation lasted three minutes. That's too short to ask a woman for her number; she's going to think I'm weird and say no.

Well, my fear won the battle that time, because I said my goodbyes to her, and we went our separate ways. Immediately after we walked away, I regretted my decision. I was thinking about running back around and asking for her contact information but realized that would be a truly stupid decision, so I said screw it and kept walking.

Even though the experience didn't end the way I wanted it to, overall it was a win for me because I learned two things. One, I approached a woman I'd never met before, and this was going to do wonders for my future confidence. Two, I now have a better sense of the personality type that I might seek in a potential partner.

I thought the story was over after that day, but it wasn't!

A few weeks later I was studying in the business faculty building at my university in between classes. A woman walked up to me and said, "Are you the guy who . . ."

I didn't even let her finish the sentence. "Yeah," I said, "I'm that guy."

It was her! Maybe God or a higher power wanted to give me a second chance to summon the courage to ask for her contact information. I'm not super religious or a believer in fate, but if that was indeed a force at play, thank you.

We had another amusing conversation, speaking for well over an hour this time.

About ten minutes into the conversation, I asked her for her number and social-media information. I wasn't going to let myself wait too long to redeem my mistake. We kept in touch for a while after that conversation, but external forces may have stopped something more from happening.

Although this is a personal example of approaching a woman, if you're a woman, you can and should feel free to approach a man you're interested in. The same principles apply regardless of gender or sexual orientation.

ASK FOR THEIR CONTACT INFORMATION

If a conversation is going well but it's coming to an end, ask for the other person's contact information—assuming you want to, of course. I can't tell you how many great interactions I have had with people where I forgot to ask for any sort of contact information. If you don't get someone's contact information—assuming that you're not in a social setting where you'll see each other again—there's a good chance you'll never have another opportunity to do so.

Asking for their contact information is the easiest part—hand out your phone and say, "Let me get your number or social-media info." Don't overthink this part—it's the easiest step. Send them a message within the day, so you stay fresh in their mind.

COMMON CONVERSATION MISTAKES

Although the basics of conversation are simple and straightforward, there are some common conversation mistakes that can derail the opportunity to be social with someone, since these mistakes typically signal a lack of social intelligence or ability.

Too Much Tension

When you're speaking to someone for the first time, there may be a great deal of tension, especially on the receiving side, since you are a stranger who came up to them out of the blue. This is less of a problem if you're at a social event, since there is an inherent sense of familiarity, but it's a common issue if you're talking to people randomly.

Unless you do something to ease the tension at the start of the conversation, the threat factor won't disappear, which might cause the other person to stay guarded and potentially look to leave the conversation as soon as possible.

This is why smiling is so important; smiling immediately drops the potential threat level down. Pair this with the following tactic for calm, casual transitions into conversation.

When entering a conversation, do something to acknowledge the fact that this is a random conversation and you're a stranger. This will help the person with whom you're speaking realize you're socially intelligent enough to be aware of the situation and to ease the tension. Those who lack social intelligence immediately cause others to raise their guard, since a lack of social intelligence may code as a potential threat in the subconscious mind.

Effective opening lines include:

- "Hey, sorry to bother you, but . . ."
- "I know this is kind of random, but . . ."
- "Hey, this is completely out of the blue, but . . ."

If the situation allows for it, you can also add in what you are going to be doing in the future. This will show the other person there is a time limit to the conversation. The two things that people worry about when a person randomly starts a conversation with them are: "Are they a threat?" and "How can I leave?" By smiling and acknowledging the randomness of your meeting, you diminish the threat factor. Communicating that you have a time limit helps to ease the other person's tension, as they can be assured that this conversation is going to come to an end soon. We've all had conversations where we've just met another person and they don't know how to take the hint that we wanted to end the conversation and move on. Making people feel trapped in a conversation with a person they don't know isn't a great ingredient for social success. Whether you and the other person vibe and continue the conversation is up to you both, but at least the other person will know you're not a threat.

The following recommendations are optional and context-dependent. I hope they will help you out, but don't force a reason if you don't have one.

- **At a mall, introducing yourself to a person:** "Pardon me, I was just about to head into the store, but I wanted to say you have a really cool jacket."
- **At a social event, introducing yourself to a person:** "Hey there, I was just about to head over there with my friends, but I couldn't help but overhear you were a big Lakers fan—so am I."
- **At a bar, introducing yourself to a person:** "Hey, sorry to bother you; I was just about to get a drink, but I noticed you from over there, and I wanted to say hi."

Outcome-Focused

A big problem that many people make when interacting with others is they are too focused on an outcome, such as being liked, getting contact information, or making a new friend. If you're too focused on an outcome, then you're not focused on what actually makes the outcome possible. This can make you nervous and self-conscious, as your participation and enjoyment of the conversation is dependent on signals the other individual gives and/or the result that follows.

There isn't anything wrong with trying to achieve an outcome, but that shouldn't be the motivating factor behind your interactions. When you're interacting in a social setting (versus in the context of business or a formal occasion), your goal should be to have fun and find out what's interesting about the other person. Combine this goal with the steps we've discussed and with what we'll continue to discuss throughout this book—like feeling comfortable and positive, being respectable, being vulnerable, and developing social intelligence. By doing so, the outcomes you want will usually come as a natural byproduct.

Worrying about Running Out of Things to Say

"How can I not run out of things to say?" is a common concern for those who are trying to learn how to start conversations with new people. Being concerned about running out of things to say is the wrong thing to worry about. You can never "run out" of things to say, as there is an endless number of topics you can talk about.

The underlying concern of the question "How can I not run out of things to say?" is digging at another question: "How can I be more comfortable with this person?" Do you ever run out of things to say with people you're the most comfortable with? You most likely don't. When a topic of conversation seems to be ending and one of you wants to keep the conversation going, you say something else—it's that easy. There isn't a concern of "Am I saying the right thing?"—you say what you want because you're comfortable enough to do so. The only caveat here is that you're knowledgeable enough to have topics you can talk about, but most of you are more knowledgeable in communicating than you believe.

Not Touching

Although humans communicate with words, they also need to connect through touch. Touch is one of the most primal ways we connect. Being touched signals companionship. Positive, respectful, consensual touch communicates safety and trust. Who do you let touch you, and who do you touch? The answer is: people who are close to you. Friends, family, significant others. Who do you not let touch you? The answer is: anyone you haven't yet registered as safe. This includes strangers (to an extent), or people who don't make you feel comfortable and secure.

You must be conscious of how you use touch. Too little may make you seem like a distant acquaintance, and too much uncalibrated touch may make you seem off-putting and/or socially incompetent. A safe rule is to stick with handshakes, shoulder pats, upper back pats, and quick hugs for those you are not intimate with.

Forgetting the Name

Remember to use people's names. The easiest way to make someone really like you is to remember and use their name. The easiest way to turn someone off is to forget their name and refer to them as "man," "dude," "girl," etc.

When people say they're bad at names, they're indicating one of two things. The first is poor memory recall, which can be a signal for poor health or low general intelligence. Either that, or they didn't put in the effort of remembering someone's name. Most times, it's the latter, and this is exactly why using someone's name makes them like you more—it's essentially an investment in them.

To help you better remember people's names, try to activate three forms of memory: audio, visual, and verbal. Hear their name, see their name, and say their name. Listening to their name, repeating it in conversation, then getting contact information hit all three forms of memory.

The World Is Full of People You Can Meet

The world is full of people. Once you're able to talk to and meet new people, life opens up to you in ways you would've never been able to imagine before. Every person has the potential to open up opportunities in us that were previously inaccessible.

THROUGH WORK

If you work a full-time job, you're most likely going to be spending anywhere from thirty to fifty hours a week with your colleagues. Are the people you work with people you actively want to be friends with or people who you actively avoid and despise? Remember, the data on friendships suggests that we may need to spend about two hundred hours with someone to consider them a close friend, and work is likely the way that's going to happen for many people.

If you're about to start a new job, put in some thought about who you're going to work with. These people are going to be among the top reasons for your happiness (or misery). If you have a choice between working a job where you get to interact with great people or working a job in an empty office building that pays more than the former, it would be a good idea to put a lot of thought into your decision and consider the impact of both situations on your day-to-day life. If you currently work with people you can't stand, it may be worth changing where you work.

OUT AND ABOUT

Start to notice the people around you on a day-to-day basis as actual people and not background characters to your life story. The people around you might include:

- The barista when you get your morning coffee
- The people standing in line or at the coffee shop
- The person you sit next to on the bus or train
- The group beside you at the bar
- The person working out next to you at the gym
- The trainer or manager at the gym
- The waiter or waitress who is serving you
- The people waiting at the crosswalk
- The person in the same aisle at the grocery store
- The people in your group activity
- The people in your office building

Noticing the people around you as actual people instantly snaps you back into reality. Oftentimes, we live in our own bubble. It can sometimes feel like the people we hang out with and the people we follow on social media are the only people in our lives, but that is not the case.

SOCIAL EVENTS

Social events are arguably the best place to meet new people. A group of people doing something together or gathered in a place for a specific reason automatically reduces the stranger-danger aspect, as you have a built-in reason to talk to each other.

Almost all social gatherings have some built-in form of socializing, whether it be icebreakers, networking activities, or the gathering itself. Social events are a great way to engage in social situations where starting a conversation is easy, since these gatherings are meant to foster interactions with other people. It may still be scary, but it will be far less scary than trying to start conversations with people out and about.

Almost all cities and towns have some sort of group events available, whether they be a sports league, classes, meetup groups, or volunteering. With internet platforms being so widely available, these events can be easy to find, but it's on you to seek them out and attend.

FRIENDS OF FRIENDS

Friends of friends take the benefits of social events and magnify them. When you meet a friend of a friend, not only is the threat of stranger danger diminished, it's almost eliminated because your friend has already screened the other person for you (assuming that they're a friend that you both respect).

The best thing about meeting friends of friends is that you can all do things together. This will help you have more social support and can reduce the pressure of meeting even more new people at social events or gatherings.

Social-Effort Leverage

If you're going to put in the effort to create your social life, you might as well leverage your efforts. You can do this by creating a lifestyle that allows you to be social and develop relationships. When you put in the effort to create a more social lifestyle, you'll likely find that it becomes easier to be social. You will already be in social situations, and all you have to do is open your mouth and talk.

WORK LIFE

If you're going to spend the majority of your waking hours working, recognize that work is the best place to start building your social life. It's easy to neglect work as an avenue to a good social life because if you're like me, work is work, but having a good social life at work does wonders for job performance, your happiness, and the performance and happiness of others. Being at a job where you don't have friends or don't talk to anyone sucks—I've been there.

Don't Take Coffee Breaks Alone

If you're going to refill your coffee mug or make your way down to the cafe to get a cup, bring someone. Make it a habit to bring someone as often as possible.

You can talk about work, your personal lives, or any other topic that you or they want to talk about. This opens the door for longer, better conversations at a different time. Coffee-break chats are a great time for you to invite your coworkers to sit with you at lunch, get a drink after work, or attend an event on the weekend.

Don't Eat Lunch at Your Desk

The first company I worked for—a successful local startup—had a rule: you can't eat lunch at your desk. The rule made sense, because eating lunch with a group of your colleagues gives you an hour or so of talking time that doesn't require you to talk about work. Some of the best interactions I've had have come from the lunch table. It brought a unique type of joy to my day to talk about sports, crack jokes, get to know my colleagues, and exchange some off-the-wall topics with them. As the company grew and people got busier, they stopped implementing this rule, which is a shame, because it was such a great one.

Is a Hotdog a Sandwich?

"Hey, is a hotdog a sandwich?" This is a question that I heard someone ask during a lunch break. To other people, this may be a question that sparks a bit of thought and then concludes with an answer, but that wasn't the case for us. If you get ten to fifteen loud, young, smart men and women involved in a debate, it's going to be an hour-long war, with the lunch table as the battleground.

We argued about everything. Does the fact that it's a piece of meat and condiments between bread make it a sandwich? Does it have to have two separate pieces of bread to be called a sandwich? What kind of bread determines a sandwich? Soon enough, we Googled it, and according to the internet, yes, a hotdog can be considered a sandwich because a sandwich is "two or more slices of bread or a split roll having a filling in between"—although if you asked some of my former coworkers today, they may give you an answer contrary to that theory.

I Bet I Can Beat a Horse in a Marathon

Same company, different lunchtime debate—yes, we got work done, too; don't worry. One man, "Stewart," was always coming up with wacky thoughts and ideas that were highly entertaining but usually questionable. The best example of this is when Stewart claimed he could beat a horse in a marathon. He knew a horse would be far faster than him, but he wondered if a horse could realistically run forty-two kilometers before he could. Personally, I was wondering if he could run forty-two kilometers at all . . .

Turns out they do man-versus-horse marathons every year, and horses win almost every time. So, Stewart is going to have to hang onto his dreams of beating a horse in a race. It would be funny if it was man versus horse in the Kentucky Derby, but that wouldn't be fair.

The importance of lunchtime socializing became obvious to me when I worked at a second company, another successful local startup. The leaders there implemented no such lunchtime rule, so people typically ate lunch at their desks while working. The whole day often felt like a drag if I didn't make my own efforts to socialize because I'd be at my desk all day with little interaction.

If your company has no such rule, you can take the initiative to start it or at least execute it at an individual level. Start with one or a small group of people. Invite them to have lunch with you. Then invite the quieter, shier people once you've established a lunchtime group. Soon enough, you'll have a big group of people who now have one hour of great socializing, connections, and joy injected into their workday. You can bet that their morale and yours will go up, and maybe even their job performance and contribution to the company too.

The most important thing is to stay consistent. If you're going to do this daily, make it daily. If it's a once or twice a week thing, pick a day and stick to it.

I cannot say this enough: do not underestimate the power of lunchtime socializing. Getting one hour a day to socialize five times a week will help you develop some of the best connections you'll have. If you're a manager or a company leader and you don't have lunchtime gatherings implemented at your office, do it now. You're wasting a perfectly good opportunity to build company culture and boost morale in a way that you won't be able to replicate otherwise.

If you work in an office with other people, this is the most optimal place to create social connections. This by no means requires you to take focus away from your job or stop working hard—in fact, it's the opposite. When you are happy in your workplace, you tend to work harder and do better work. As long as your conversations don't interrupt your job or that of others, social interactions should be a key part of your workday.

If you're not in an office—whether you work in a store, job site, warehouse, or so on—it's still possible to be social within your work environment. You'll have to understand your specific situation to make the most of it, since a retail clothing store, for example, will be much different from a construction site, but if you take the right steps and stick with them, you'll always have an opportunity to socialize with your coworkers.

Remote-Work Social Life

Remote work can make social interactions more challenging, since you are all in your own houses working on your own, with social connection coming through online channels such as video chat or team messaging systems, but you can make do with what you have. For the most satisfying connection, you'll want to use video-conferencing software as much as possible, since text-based communication doesn't allow for the same type of human experience.

If you're a leader of a team that works remotely or are an employee who wants to bring up new ideas, consider the following:

- Ten-minute video-chat breaks multiple times a day. There are a number of apps that can facilitate this, but a manual video-conference schedule works well, too.
- Designated video-chat lunch hours. If you don't have this as a company, start now!
- After-work socials. We're saving everyone commute time with remote work. Why not host a social to fill that time? You can host a simple video-conference social or drinks event, or you can even host virtual game nights.
- Encourage employees to work outside their houses. Coffee shops, libraries, or a friend/family's place works great.
- Have physical meetups with your team members regularly. Lunch/dinners, playing sports, going hiking, or getting drinks all work fantastic.
- Offer counseling/therapy as a perk. Seriously! Working at home for forty or more hours a week can affect your employees' mental health, since they will have fewer social interactions and possibly more stress. Beyond that, it's overall a good practice to take care of the people who work for you.

WHAT DO YOU DO AFTER WORK?

After work is a great time to be social with a colleague because the workday is done, you've put in a lot of effort, and you want to relax. It doesn't need to be anything big, like a dinner or drinks, although those are nice options. If hanging out in the office after work or going to the coffee shop across the street is more your style, then go for it! It definitely beats being at home on your phone or computer, doesn't it?

Although being in an office is ideal for creating a social life, as you'll be in closer proximity to a large group of people, a work-based social life can still be possible if you work at a job site or from home.

OUT-OF-HOUSE LIFESTYLE

Almost all social events will require you to leave your house and go to another place, and most opportunities to meet people will require the same. This is why you need to start building the habit of not being in your house all the time, which is actually a problem many people struggle with quite a bit.

Even if you don't have any social activities planned, make it a habit to get out of your house anyway. One, it will get you in the right state of mind to be outside instead of hermit-crabbed indoors all day, and two, it may create new avenues to meet people. You could meet someone while you're out, or you could find a new place to meet new people.

By a similar token, make it a habit not to use your phone or be plugged into your headphones when you're out. This makes it extremely difficult to talk to people spontaneously and it keeps you in your own bubble of isolation.

Ways you can be out of the house more include:

- Doing work at a coffee shop
- Visiting the gym
- Playing sports

- Going for a run
- Biking
- Taking a walk through a park or through your city/town
- Explore a new part of your city/town
- Hiking
- Walking a pet
- Volunteering
- Enjoying yoga
- Attending free social events
- Engaging in outdoor hobbies

Actively Find Social Activities

Make an active effort to find social activities, whether you do so through online platforms or by keeping an eye out for activities in town.

When you're invited to social activities, follow my rule: unless you have a really good reason not to attend, go!

Don't limit yourself to finding things to do—engaging in a social activity could mean creating one yourself. Everyone wants to go to events to have fun and meet new people, but few people are willing to lead and organize an event. Be the person who brings the fun to your friends. Your social life strategy should look to create as many social events as you attend. Group situations are golden! When you don't know people too well and they don't know you too well either, one-on-one events can lead to a lot of pressure, especially if the participants are not used to this type of interaction. Group situations help relieve some of that stress. You'll also have the added benefit of being able to be social with multiple people at once.

WHO DO YOU LIVE WITH?

The person or people you live with have a big impact on your social life because they're likely the ones you socialize with most on a daily basis, unless your life outside your house is exceptionally social.

Do the people you live with drain your energy, or do they bring you joy? Do you try to avoid your living companions, or do you actively go out of your way to talk to them? Do you feel like you belong in your living conditions, or do you feel trapped and lonely?

Deliberately picking the people you live with will be paramount to your daily social fulfillment and happiness.

As a general rule, similar to the friends you're going to be investing your time and effort into, choose to live with kind, considerate, respectful, fun, and interesting people you get along with.

The problem with living with people you dislike is that the quality of your daily experience drops significantly, since you will be at home for a decent portion of your days and moving out and finding a new place to live is a lengthy and often stressful process.

Here are a number of common living situations that can cause problems:

- Moving into an apartment/house without knowing the other people in the house well
- Moving in with your boyfriend/girlfriend if your relationship isn't trending toward marriage
- Moving into a place only because the rent is cheap
- Having a crowded house
- Having a lonely house
- Having bad neighbors, especially if you live in an apartment or in close quarters
- Raising your kids poorly

- Moving into a bad part of town
- Living with people who sleep at significantly different times from you
- Living with people who you don't like. If you don't like them before you move in, it will magnify when you move in with them. (Sounds obvious, but I have to put it in here.)
- Living with people who have significantly different life attitudes from you
- Living with people who have significantly different levels of conscientiousness from you. (Work ethic, cleanliness, orderliness, etc.)
- Living with people who have significantly different noise preferences
- Living with people who have significantly different guest quantities
- Living with people who are negative or pessimistic
- Living with your parents, if you don't like living with them
- Living with your extended family, if you don't like living with them
- Living with people who cannot take negativity or constructive criticism well
- Living with people who cannot communicate their problems effectively

Do what you can to avoid those situations in order to make your social life at home become one that brings you joy and energizes you, not one that you dread and brings you down.

Key Takeaways

- Unless you already have potential people with whom you can be good friends, your future friendships are going to come from people you haven't yet met.
- When you talk to new people, smile often to signal friendliness, open conversations before your mental blocks convince you not to, start conversations effectively, and avoid common conversational mistakes.
- Excellent ways to meet new people include: through work, out and about, at social events, and via friends of friends.
- Creating a lifestyle in which you're consistently exposed to social opportunities is a great way to leverage your effort.

CHAPTER 5

Vulnerability—The Key to Social Success

It's a Sunday afternoon when I make my way to my university gym like usual. It's about 1:00 p.m., and the gym is pretty empty aside from a staff member and a few people getting their workout in. I head over to warm up on the bike before getting in a solid full body workout. Then I see her. And by her, I mean one of the most gorgeous women I've ever seen. Tall, slim, long hair, with a beautiful face.

I've never really approached a woman I found attractive until that point. I've approached some women that I wasn't too attracted to, although those instances almost always ended poorly for me. I've also experienced enough moments where I let opportunities pass, and the feeling of regret is worse than any rejection, so this time, I go for it. When I make the decision to approach this woman, I jump out of my seat and make my move.

I walk over to the free weight area where she is working out and sit down next to her. I was already planning to exercise there, anyway. I turn to her and ask her what she's working on. She smiles and tells me shoulders and arms. I tell her that's pretty cool and crack a joke. She laughs. I ask her what she's studying at the university and she responds, "Science."

Then she asks me what I study, and I ask her to guess. Giving straight answers is boring sometimes. The first guess she gives is engineering. I should've seen this coming because I'm an Asian man with a slightly nerdy appearance.

She fails a few more times, so I tell her I'm a business student. I make another joke because it's a running joke at my university that everybody hates the business faculty—I don't blame them. She assures me that she doesn't hate me because of what I study. She also tells me that she doesn't know anyone from business, so I tell her I'm honored to be the first one!

At this point, I figure I should introduce myself. I do and ask for her name in return. She tells me her name is "Stacey." Then I launch what is arguably my favorite line. I'm not one for pickup lines or memorizing what to say beforehand—I think that interrupts the natural flow and fun of the conversation—but I've been dying to use this one.

"Nice to meet you, Stacey. If I'm going to be honest, I thought you were really cute, and I just had to come over and say hi."

She looks at me shocked, like I just offered to pay off her student loans or something. She smiles, and I lose my train of thought.

At that moment, I notice she has really pretty eyes, so I guess we're both admiring something about each other.

We chat for a bit more, but now she's totally stunned and is giving me her complete attention.

We talk for a bit more, then I ask for her number, but she tells me she has a boyfriend. Damn it!

I tell her to take it as a compliment, smile, and get back to my workout. For some reason, I don't feel bad at all. I'm still super happy with myself.

It definitely wasn't one of those "I have a boyfriend" manners of blowing me off. I knew she was being honest because I saw her a few times after that with her man . . . Lucky guy!

What if you could walk up to anyone and start a conversation without the fear of rejection stopping you?

What if you could go to social events without fear holding you back?

What if you could share the secret you've always wanted to get off your chest without worrying about coming across as weak?

What if all this was actually possible and not just a series of imaginary, rhetorical questions?

It is!

Express Your Truth

If there was one key factor that could change your social life, it would be vulnerability.

When you hear the word vulnerability, you may think of weakness—for example, a person sobbing over their feelings. While this is a form of vulnerability, it is not entirely what we're discussing here.

Think of vulnerability more generally in a way that includes physical, social, and emotional vulnerability. Vulnerability can be better defined as being willing to express your truth. Express your truth by being vulnerable, and accept the uncertainty that comes with it.

The reason vulnerability is so important and yet so difficult for people to express is because of uncertainty. Humans are creatures of habit and certainty. We create habits and lifestyles that are familiar to us, we attach meaning to things so we can feel a sense of certainty, and we rush to close any mental gaps we may be experiencing (this is why cliffhangers are so effective at getting you to watch the next episode). These practices come from survival instincts.

Unfortunately, the same survival instincts that got us and our ancestors to this point can also play against our true desires. This is why vulnerability is key. Everyone has true desires—whether it's wanting to go to the party we were invited to, wanting to walk up to someone we don't know and start a conversation with them, or wanting to share a secret with a person we trust. In any of these situations, vulnerability is crucial. It helps us to overcome the uncertainty that our basic human instinct doesn't want any part of.

There are three types of vulnerability: physical, social, and emotional. While all of these types share the same concept of expressing your truth, they also come with different fears and uncertainties.

PHYSICAL VULNERABILITY

Being vulnerable can include being physically vulnerable. This in no way means you should put yourself in dangerous or risky situations, but it does mean you'll need to step out of your comfort zone physically in order to express your true desires.

Expressing your truth physically could mean that instead of coming straight home from work, you arrange a dinner with a friend. Your truth is that you want to take the time to meet with a friend to develop your friendship instead of going home where it's comfortable. Being vulnerable enough to attend a dinner with a friend is your way of expressing your true desire.

Going to a social event is another way to express your truth through physical vulnerability. Perhaps you want to attend a party hosted by your coworker this weekend, but you're hesitant because you don't know everyone there and big groups of people make you nervous. Physical vulnerability comes into play here because if you do go in spite of your fears and in spite of the uncertainty of what could happen, you are being vulnerable and expressing your true desire.

If you're going to improve your social life, physical vulnerability is a must. Almost all of the things you need to do in order to create a social life you enjoy will involve you physically being somewhere.

Unfortunately, our technology-focused, isolation-driven culture has turned many of us into hermit-crab-type humans, where we prefer to stay home due to the comfort and convenience. But we're likely not going to make friends by staying at home.

Other examples of being physically vulnerable to express your truth include:

- Leaving the house when you've spent all day being inside
- Going to a social event
- Hosting a social
- Signing up for a class and attending
- Moving to another city

- Meeting up with a friend
- Going on a first date
- Getting drinks after work with a coworker

The Social Safety Valve

Here is a great adage you can implement to help alleviate some of the uncertainty that comes from physical vulnerability: you can always go home.

A big anxiety that comes from making yourself physically vulnerable is your exit plan. How will you get home? If you allow yourself the opportunity to excuse yourself and go home anytime you want, you'll always have a path of safety. With ride-hailing services being so inexpensive and widely available, it's become a lot easier and cheaper to go home from anywhere, at any time.

Most of the time, this mindset benefits you. Because you know that you can go home at any time, you feel more relaxed during social events. When you feel relaxed, you're more likely to be in a positive headspace and are more likely to project that headspace outward. Giving yourself the option to go home at any time can actually make you enjoy being there far more—try it next time you make yourself physically vulnerable.

I Released the Safety Valve

One summer, my coworker invited me to his place for Canada Day. He lived in the student neighborhood of my city, so inviting me to his place more or less meant hanging out outside his house, sipping beers with groups of people, and interacting with other people doing the same. I knew my coworker, although I wasn't close with him. I wasn't going to know anybody else in attendance. If this isn't an example of physical vulnerability, I don't know what is.

I wanted to go, but my concerns were probably similar to the ones that you've experienced countless times, too. What if I don't meet anyone cool there? What if I end up sitting by myself? What if I look like an idiot? But when I thought those thoughts, I told myself, "You can always go home." If I wanted to leave, I could say my goodbyes to my coworker and walk home. It wouldn't be a big deal. Knowing this was enough to convince me to attend.

It turned out to be exactly as I'd feared. After chatting with my coworker for a bit, I spent the majority of the time sitting by myself, sipping beers, and watching other groups of people chat. I got in some socializing when a beer pong game started, although my inexperience at the game and not knowing anyone at the table deterred me from talking much.

After an hour or so of sitting around alone and awkwardly, I released the safety valve and decided to head home. It wasn't a big deal. I went to the event and took a chance, but ultimately it wasn't a great experience.

These things happen, especially if you're learning how to be social and have just started attending events. It was a valuable lesson in being able to go to events freely and having an option to leave at any point. Since then, I have attended countless events where I extended the same line to myself, but ultimately ended up staying and enjoying the event way more than I would have without a backup plan.

SOCIAL VULNERABILITY

Social vulnerability is when you make yourself vulnerable through communication in order to express your truth. The main obstacle that you're seeking to overcome is the uncertainty of whether people like you.

Expressing your truth socially could mean going up to a person you don't know and starting a conversation with them. The truth you are trying to express here is your desire to speak to this person. The uncertainty that comes with it is of not knowing how this person will react to you. Will they like you? Will they be annoyed you interrupted them? Will they become your best friend? No matter the outcome, by being socially vulnerable, you are able to accept the uncertainty that comes with expressing your desires.

This example isn't limited to people you don't know. The same stands for people you already know. These people may be friends of yours, but you may still experience uncertainty when you want to start a conversation with them. This is why many people have trouble starting a conversation, inviting other people out, or being the one to text first.

Other forms of social vulnerability include telling a joke that may not be funny, expressing an opinion that people may not agree with, or changing the topic of a conversation. All of these forms of social vulnerability create uncertainty because you don't know how the other person may react—however, going through any one of these motions will help you express yourself more.

When you hold back an opinion or a topic of interest you want to talk about, you give in to your own fears of uncertainty. You restrict yourself from developing strong relationships with people because you don't let people get to know you. Many people hold back on sharing their opinions or topics of interest because they don't want people not to like them. This fear-based justification often backfires because playing it safe prevents people from loving us for who we are. People can't truly love us if we don't share our deeper thoughts and feelings with them.

Other examples of social vulnerability can include:

- Introducing yourself to someone you've never met
- Inviting someone to hangout
- Texting first
- Asking someone on a date
- Suggesting a place to meet up
- Giving a compliment
- Sharing a controversial opinion

Most of the time, people won't react in the negative way that you may think they will. Unless they're terrible people or what you've said is bad or offensive, most people will either respond with neutrality or positivity.

But there is a bigger value than that. Being socially vulnerable means expressing who you truly are in terms of your thoughts, feelings, and desires. Social vulnerability is an integral part of building relationships with others.

EMOTIONAL VULNERABILITY

When people think of vulnerability, they usually think of emotional vulnerability. Emotional vulnerability is concerned with expressing or revealing the parts of yourself that aren't your most flattering aspects or attributes.

Hold up . . . What?

Why on earth would anyone want to show parts of themselves that can make them look bad?

This may be a valid concern for people, especially young people. We're so used to sharing only the good parts of our lives and posting only the highlights of our best days on social media. Why in the world would we ever want to expose the parts of ourselves that we're not proud of?

The simple answer? Connection. We don't connect over images of perfection, we connect through understanding one another's whole selves, and this includes the parts that we're not proud of—our shortcomings.

Emotional vulnerability is by far the most confusing and complex of the three different types of vulnerability. You might wonder:

- *Won't people think I'm a loser?*
- *Won't people take advantage of me?*
- *Won't people lose respect for me?*
- *Will people perceive me as being weak?*

There's no clean, pretty answer to those questions, but let's take a look at the different forms that emotional vulnerability can take.

Emotional Fort Knoxers

These people are extremely emotionally invulnerable. They guard their emotions and any sense of negative perception like how the United States guards Fort Knox—no one is getting in there.

I feel for those people. The reason why people are emotionally guarded is they don't know how to express their emotions or they're protecting themselves from pain, usually subconsciously.

Of course, they have a responsibility to work through their issues, but they're probably dealing with difficult things, even though they won't tell anyone about it.

Emotional Fort Knoxers usually don't have very close friends in their lives. This doesn't mean they don't have people to hang out with or don't know people—they could—but chances are they don't know them well, and vice versa. These people can be highly respected due to other circumstances, such as having a successful career, being talented, being social, and so on, but they are likely lacking in terms of an intimate friendship. Chances are, while other people may not judge them, they most likely judge themselves quite harshly.

If you feel like you share similar traits to Fort Knoxers, working through your mental patterns with a professional therapist can be a good idea. Although this may be hard for them to hear because they may not want to admit they have a problem in the first place (since looking weak is the cause of their problems), this is precisely the reason why they may need to seek help in one way or another.

Everyone hates looking weak. Nobody wants to look stupid or feel ashamed of themselves, but if someone is struggling with feelings of inadequacy to the extent that they're not willing to open up about their feelings at all, they are likely experiencing an issue that will be difficult to work out on their own.

Emotional Weeper

Emotional weepers are one step ahead of emotional Fort Knoxers because they're at least willing to reveal their emotions and feelings. Emotional weepers are openly down and sad, while emotional Fort Knoxers are down and sad in a closed-off way.

I feel for emotional weepers as well. Although they are probably in a better position, as they don't suffer in silence or put on fake acts of happiness, they likely have difficult things in their lives, whether they're consciously aware of them or not. Unfortunately, when the emotional weeper doesn't deal with these problems, other people (especially happy, ambitious, successful people) may not be too keen on interacting beyond a surface level.

The solution for emotional weepers is the same as the one for emotional Fort Knoxers—get professional help. There is definitely something—or many things—at the root of the problem that the emotional weeper probably isn't consciously aware of.

Emotional Vomitter

Emotional vomitters are people who may be decently emotional and socially stable. However, when they get an opportunity to be emotionally vulnerable, they go way too overboard. TMI! Too much information!

At one point, I was guilty of being an emotional vomitter. It wasn't uncommon for me to overshare with people whom I barely knew. Understandably, these people wanted to run away from me as fast as they could.

Emotional vomitters are doing one thing that may take emotional Fort Knoxers and emotional weepers a lot of time to figure out—they're being vulnerable. The problem is, instead of adding a drop of vulnerability to an interaction to make it richer and more fulfilling, they dump in the whole bucket.

Emotional vomiting can be caused by one of two things—either an emotional problem or a tactical problem.

If an emotional vomitter is suffering from an emotional problem, this means they'll release all of their feelings on the person to whom they're speaking, which burdens that person. If the recipient of the emotional vomit is extremely patient, this situation can be fine, but emotional vomitters may be advised to talk to someone about their oversharing, whether it be a professional therapist or a trusted friend or a family member who has experience dealing with them.

Emotional vomitters can also suffer due to a tactical problem. They may not have emotional problems that cause them to emotionally vomit, but they may not logically understand how to go about sharing their emotions. If this is the case, they can simply wait until an appropriate time to release their feelings or gradually release them over time to build some sense of familiarity to these problems.

Emotionally Strong and Vulnerable

Ideally, you'll want to stay emotionally strong while being vulnerable. When you're emotionally strong and vulnerable, you project both power and humility. You communicate that you're strong enough to share the negative aspects of yourself, yet humble enough to do so. When someone is emotionally strong, they are also socially intelligent when sharing with others. They start off by sharing smaller and less emotionally significant vulnerabilities, and as they establish trust and friendship, they gradually address deeper topics. This helps them build authentic connections over time. Emotionally strong and vulnerable people don't burden new people with emotional explosions.

Plus, they understand that whomever they're speaking to may not be capable of processing such intense emotions until they become better acquainted.

Vulnerability Baby Steps

All babies must learn how to crawl before they can walk on two feet. When they figure out their hands don't need to be on the ground to transport themselves, their ambition to walk on two feet is usually met with many stumbles and wobbly steps—and the guidance of worried parents.

The best way to develop any new habits, including emotional ones, is to build them gradually through systematic desensitization. Systematic desensitization is a type of behavioral therapy that helps people overcome phobias or build behaviors through incremental progress—in baby steps. The opposite of this method is called flooding, which seeks to completely overhaul your behavioral patterns by exposing you to the extreme end in a sudden manner. For example, if someone is terrified of flying, putting them into an airplane would be an example of flooding. If this person was instead asked to visualize themselves getting onto an airplane, or watched a video of passengers in an airplane, this would be the first step in systematic desensitization. While both of these methods make sense in theory—in practice, systematic desensitization is far more effective for long-lasting change.

SYSTEMATIC DESENSITIZATION

Systematic desensitization can be used to help with vulnerability. The goal of this method is to take incremental steps towards your end goal. This way, each step along the way is doable and doesn't require a giant emotional shift, although it certainly takes consistent effort over time.

When you have a vulnerability goal you want to reach, do this exercise:

1. Write down what you ideally want to achieve.
2. Write down where you are currently.
3. Create one to five incremental steps that will help you progress towards your ideal goal.
4. Write down the challenges you perceive yourself facing and how you can overcome them.

SYSTEMATIC DESENSITIZATION EXAMPLES:

Physical Vulnerability

1. Ideal goal: *Be able to have fun and be comfortable at a party*
2. Where I am now: *Nervous in groups*
    - Additional information to make a better example: *currently comfortable in one-on-one interactions*
3. Progressive steps:
    a. *Get comfortable putting myself into groups. Just put myself in a group, and don't worry about anything else for now.*
    b. *Get comfortable contributing to group interactions. Study group-conversation dynamics if I need to.*
    c. *Get comfortable expressing myself better in groups.*
    d. *Say yes to the next party I get invited to.*
4. Perceived challenges and solutions:
    a. *Feeling awkward about looking like I'm not contributing to the interaction*
        i. *Focus on the interaction, not myself.*

   b. *Feeling embarrassed saying or doing something stupid*
      i. *Laugh it off or joke about it if it's not something with bad intentions.*
      ii. *Apologize if necessary.*
      iii. *Move on to another topic of conversation; practice self-acceptance.*

Social Vulnerability

1. Ideal goal: *Being able to be the one to ask a friend to hang out.*
2. Where I am now: *I want to hang out with people, but I'm too nervous to ask. I'm comfortable hanging out with people, however.*
3. Progressive steps:
   a. *Start with people who are safe: family and close friends.*
   b. *Start text conversations with people I want to hang out with (real conversations if face-to-face).*
   c. *Make the ask.*
4. Perceived challenges and solutions:
   a. *Fear of rejection*
      i. *Ask myself what this rejection means. Do I think this person doesn't like me because they rejected me? Does this person's opinion of me dictate my perception of self?*
   b. *Uncertainty waiting for a text back*
      i. *Practice mindfulness.*
      ii. *Put my phone away, and do something else.*
      iii. *Ask myself what is the worst that can happen?*

Emotional Vulnerability

1. Ideal goal: *Wanting to tell someone that I appreciate them as a person*
2. Where I am now: *Can have conversations with this person but can't be emotionally vulnerable enough*
3. Progressive steps:
    a. *Start with people who are safe: family and close friends. Try telling them that I appreciate them.*
    b. *Study how to give compliments if needed.*
    c. *Get into a deeper conversation with this person.*
    d. *Pay them the compliment.*
4. Perceived challenges and solutions:
    a. *This person may not react well and could embarrass me.*
        i. *Be mindful that that is more a reflection of them and their emotional capacity, and not a reflection of who I am.*

When I want to develop the skill of talking to people I've never met, my systematic desensitization process looks something like this.

1. Ideal goal: *Be able to approach a person and have a fun, engaging conversation with them*
2. Where I am now: *Can have good, fun conversations with friends I know but not people I've never met*
3. Progressive steps:
    a. *Start conversations with low-risk people such as cashiers, waiters, staff members, and people in my office.*

   - b. *Place myself in places that people I may want to talk to attend.*
   - c. *Begin conversations with people.*
   - d. *Hold fun, engaging conversations with people.*
4. Perceived challenges and solutions:
   - a. *Fear of approaching*
     - i. *Overcome it by focusing on each step before moving on.*
   - b. *Feeling awkward or embarrassed*
     - i. *Acknowledge the feeling in the moment, and go for it anyway.*
   - c. *Feeling different and standing out*
     - i. *Realize that I will have to do things that other people don't have the courage to do, and be comfortable with the feelings anyway.*

COMMON VULNERABILITY CONCERNS

Vulnerability is tough. Since being vulnerable means taking on uncertainty and humans are hardwired to hate uncertainty, it's natural there are a lot of concerns around this topic.

I'm Too Afraid of Rejection

Being afraid of rejection is normal. Seriously, it's human instinct. If anyone tells you they're not afraid of rejection, they're either lying or a psychopath who feels no emotion.

Here's the truth about getting over the fear of rejection: you need to focus on what's effective, not what's easy. When you focus on what's effective, the effective becomes easy, but it doesn't work the other way around. If you keep working on addressing your rejection-based fears, the less fear you will have and the more you will eventually achieve.

This is why we break down vulnerability goals into small, bite-sized steps. It's important that each one feels possible to achieve, but the truth of the matter is, at the end of the day, you will have to face rejection in order to get what you want.

Everyone's afraid of rejection, but the ones who are extremely afraid, to the point where it's inconceivable for them to take action, usually have one of two issues (or both). The first issue is they haven't faced rejection enough. If you don't face any fear enough, you're naturally going to continue to be afraid. The second issue is one of self-worth.

The human brain works in the opposite way of what we tend to believe. We tend to believe we are rational and that our decision-making comes as a result of a rational process. But this is not true for most decisions we make. Instead, the human brain comes to conclusions, then finds evidence to support those preexisting conclusions. We're not as logical as you may believe we are. When someone has a low self-image, their conclusion is they are not good enough, and any rejection they experience serves as evidence. However, if a person has an elevated self-image, then the rejection they experience doesn't serve as evidence, so it doesn't affect them as much.

If you're deathly afraid of rejection, chances are you're experiencing a self-worth issue. This is why you're going to have to continue to do all the self-improvement work discussed in this book—so you can develop positive self-esteem to the point where you can start putting yourself in situations where you may get rejected and being okay with it if it does happen.

Being Socially Vulnerable Seems Too Pushy

Isn't starting a conversation, texting first, or asking someone to meet up being pushy? The question for you is, is it pushy, or do you feel like it is? Of course, if you're the one to text first, start a conversation, or ask someone to meet up, you might feel pushy because you are the one taking the social risk to initiate. However, unless the social context is extremely off, what you're feeling is most likely your brain's defense mechanism against potential social and emotional risk.

Won't People Think I'm Weird If I'm Emotionally Vulnerable?

When you are being vulnerable, you're not necessarily being "weird"; you're being more of yourself. Remember, vulnerability is when you are willing to deal with the uncertainty of expressing your truth. Your truth is who you are, so if you're being vulnerable, you're being more of yourself. If, at your core, you're a weird person, so be it. What vulnerability is going to do for you is make the people who like you love you, and those who dislike you really dislike you. This happens when you're willing to polarize people by being yourself. When you go through this, you only attract people in your life that genuinely like you. Sounds like a win to me.

Emotional Vulnerability Seems Like Weakness

Emotional vulnerability is not necessarily weakness. If you're being emotionally vulnerable because you want to try and please other people and make them like you, you might be doing it for the wrong reasons. However, if you're being emotionally vulnerable in an effort to share who you are without depending on the validation of others, you're exhibiting strength.

It comes down to your intentions. If you share your feelings in an effort to make people like you, they'll likely run away, as their internal nonsense detectors will go off. But if you share feelings honestly and authentically, people will trust and respect you more. It's difficult to trick people of your true intentions. Most people will know what you're actually trying to do or will at least have some sense of it. Even if you do become really good at deception, why would you want to deceive? Authentic connection comes as a result of you being forthright, genuine, and honest.

Nobody Wants to Hear about Me Being Emotionally Vulnerable

This one can depend on the context of the social interaction. Most of the time, people will be more willing to hear about your vulnerabilities than you may think.

Consider this: If a person you knew was vulnerable with you, how would you take it? Would you appreciate that they had the courage to share? Would you trust and like them more? Who's to say that anyone else is really different?

If the goal of the interaction is something else, such as fun or business, your vulnerability may not be as accepted, since it may be inappropriate for that specific situation—but at the end of the day, all interactions are human interactions, and humans are quite receptive to vulnerability.

I'm Too Tired to Go Out and Do Things

This can be either a legitimate issue or an excuse. For most people, this is simply a justification for not wanting to be physically vulnerable. If you are truly too tired to go out and do things, you're likely experiencing a symptom of poor health, which you can get sorted by following the instructions in Chapter 6. However, don't discount that you might be using this justification to avoid your fears.

Ask yourself this: Could you do it if you really wanted to?

I'm Too Busy to Go Out and Do Things

Similar to being tired, being too busy can also be either a legitimate issue or an excuse. Most people will use this as another justification to avoid being physically vulnerable. If you're working eighty hours a week and have a family and/or other commitments, you may be genuinely busy, which can be its own problem. But for the average forty-hours-or-so-a-week worker with weekends off, this is most likely a justification.

Ask yourself this: Could you find a few hours throughout the week to go out and do things if you really wanted to?

INTRINSIC MOTIVATION

Vulnerability can be difficult, but there is one mindset shift you can implement to make vulnerability an opportunity instead of something you dread.

Take being healthy, for example. Maintaining your health requires you to be both physically and emotionally vulnerable, which many people dread doing. There are two big reasons why people fail at being healthy, even if they want to be. The first is they're not focused on building habits the right way. What many people do when they get excited about becoming healthy is to completely overhaul their diet, sign up for a gym and go five times a week, and create a ridiculous schedule with ridiculous expectations. If they instead focused on changing one meal at a time, sleeping properly, and going to the gym—say, twice a week instead of five times a week—they could be well on their way to achieving their goal.

But there is often something deeper at play. Most people usually aren't in touch with their true motivations. Their reasons for getting healthy may fall somewhere along the lines, of "I want to be fit and look good," or "I want to feel better." While that's not wrong, it's not necessarily all accurate either.

If they dug deeper and were willing to confront uncomfortable truths, they might come to the realization that they're motivated to become healthy because they don't feel attractive in their body. Do you think that core reason would motivate someone more than a vague, "I want to be fit and look good"? You bet it will.

The same principle can be applied to situations you face that require vulnerability. Why do you put yourself in these situations? Why are you willing to face uncertainty and discomfort? What do you have to gain, and what do you have to lose? Becoming conscious of your internal motivation will help you to become more willing to face the uncertainty.

Once you're in tune with your core reason for being vulnerable, uncertain situations will start to feel like opportunities instead of things you dread. This is the way it should be.

You know you've discovered your true internal motivation when you jump out of your seat with a new willingness to take on the task at hand. When you start to dig deep and confront your own uncomfortable truths, you'll find your real reason.

The Reason Is the Motivation

If a woman was standing outside a burning building and her friend dared her to run inside it, would she do it? Of course not! She would look at her friend like she was intoxicated.

If that same woman was standing outside this burning building, but this time her friend told her that her children were stuck inside the building and the fire department was twenty minutes away, what would she do? She would most likely sprint into the building to rescue her kids.

The woman didn't change; the building didn't change. The only variable between the two scenarios is the reason.

LOOKING STUPID OR FEELING EMBARRASSED

Looking stupid or feeling embarrassed are among people's biggest fears when it comes to being vulnerable. You may fully understand the concept of vulnerability and be excited to use it to express your truths, yet these fears still may be at the forefront of your mind.

"What if I go to this party and look stupid for standing by myself?"

"What if I ask someone to hang out, and they say no? I'll feel really worthless."

"What if I tell someone a secret, and they laugh in my face? I wouldn't be able to face that person again."

There are a few truths you're going to have to understand if you're going to be vulnerable enough to create your own rewarding social life.

- You will look stupid and embarrassed at times.
- You will be able to handle those negative thoughts with experience. It will become less and less of a big deal.
- Everyone fears looking stupid and feeling embarrassed and everyone experiences it too.
- Not many people will notice if you feel stupid or embarrassed. And if they do, they'll most likely forget about it after a while.
- The average scenarios where you look stupid or feel embarrassed aren't that bad.

The first thing you can do to overcome your fear of the unknown is define it. What exactly are you afraid of? Be specific. Often, when we actually try to explain what we're afraid of, we realize how silly our fears are.

If you're thinking about going to a party and are afraid of looking stupid, specifically define what you're afraid of.

- Initial thought:
    - *I'm scared of attending a party.*
- Better:
    - *I don't want to be in a situation where I am sitting by myself at this event with no way to start a conversation with anyone.*
- So what?

    - *People may look at me like I'm a loser for being at a party alone.*

The above exercise doesn't dictate how you can alleviate your fear but encourages you to come up with a solution when the situation arises. If you attend a party, unless you know a lot of people there, you're going to find yourself alone at one point or another.

Solutions for this scenario include:

- Talking to another person who is alone
- Getting into a group conversation
- Enjoying yourself when you're alone
- Placing yourself in a high-traffic area of the venue
- Move to another part of the venue
- Stepping out of the venue for a minute
- Going home

Check out the following example in which defining your fear can greatly diminish its power. In this scenario, someone wants to ask a friend to meet up but is afraid of getting rejected.

- Initial thought:
    - *I'm afraid of getting rejected.*
- Better:
    - *I'm afraid of asking this person to meet up and the feeling of not being liked if they reject me.*
- So what?
    - *They may be busy, or they may not like me. Do I expect every person that I interact with to like me? No.*

You may not experience rejection, but if you do, what is the consequence? You filtered someone out of your life who isn't receptive to you. Go find someone who will like you—there are plenty of fish in the sea.

THIS SEEMS TOO SIMPLE. ISN'T VULNERABILITY HARD?

After reading this chapter, you might be thinking that there's no way vulnerability can be this simple. You might say to yourself, "All I have to do to be more vulnerable is to break it down into a few progressive steps and act on it? Does Tak not realize how hard vulnerability can be? He's clearly an arrogant author."

Like many topics in this book, vulnerability seems simple to overcome when it's broken down into logical steps.

Remember, at the end of the day, vulnerability is about facing uncertainty to express your truth. While the steps may seem really simple (and they are), what isn't so easy is having the courage to go through them. Go at your own pace, break down the goals into even smaller tasks if you can, and be kind to yourself.

Unfortunately, when we're afraid of something, we try to overcomplicate it, so we have a "reasonable" justification as to why we can't accomplish it. It's a defense mechanism the brain has, a trick it uses. But we're not going to give the brain this option. We're going to keep it extremely simple, so your brain has no choice but to act. There is no "How do I do this?" It's only, "Do this."

It really is that simple. Once you get to the other side, you'll be able to do things with ease that would have terrified you before.

THE COURAGE TO BE YOURSELF

Ultimately, the whole point of vulnerability is to give you the courage to be yourself. When you are physically vulnerable and want to do something you desire, you do it. When you are socially vulnerable and want to communicate something, you say it. When you are emotionally vulnerable and want to reveal something, you go for it.

All of these types of vulnerabilities contribute to you being your full, most authentic self. Being yourself is a process of removing the mental blocks that hold you back from expressing yourself as you are. You'll need courage to overcome any uncertainty you may face along the way.

Key Takeaways

- Vulnerability is the key to changing your social life.
- Vulnerability is about expressing your truth. This means accepting the uncertainty that comes with it.
- Vulnerability comes in three forms: physical, social, and emotional.
- Taking progressive steps to overcome fears is the best way to become vulnerable.
- It's important to address common concerns and motivations to become vulnerable.
- Ultimately, the whole point of vulnerability is to give you the courage to be yourself—the complete, truthful version of yourself.

CHAPTER 6

Optimize Your Body

Driving before 1998 was terrible. Although car accidents and related injuries are unfortunately still present today, they are nothing compared to the nightmare roads that predated 1998. Regulatory bodies introduced a licensing system in the 1930s. Before that, anybody could drive a metal torpedo on wheels if they could get their hands on one. Although the licensing system surely rid the roads of some bad drivers, it still wasn't enough to keep people safe and productive in their cars. In the 1950s, universities started crash testing cars, and their findings were shocking. They found out that bad accidents and injuries weren't just the driver's fault—the cars weren't built to withstand nor to protect their passengers from such incidents. After automobile manufacturers got their hands on these reports, they went to work. Volvo was the first manufacturer to introduce the three-point seatbelt into their cars, and instantly, survival rates in car accidents increased by 50 percent. It wasn't until 1998 that the US government made it mandatory to have airbags in the front seat, which also contributed to the safety of the drivers.

Although we now might laugh at the ignorance of foolish drivers who attempted to drive cars with obvious mechanical flaws, many of us are doing the same thing socially.

At the most basic of human levels, who you are is a result of your health. Health is about how well your body is working in the way it was meant to work. When your body is working properly, you feel energized, motivated, and happy. When your body is not working properly, energy, motivation, and happiness don't happen—or at least not for long. Your brain and body need to be working how they're supposed to in order for you to get the maximum output from your social life, and your life in general.

It's extremely difficult to be socially successful for a meaningful period of time if your body isn't working in the way it was meant to. To be social, you need to be energetic, confident, mentally sharp, happy, and motivated. These things come when your body works in the way it was meant to work (i.e., when you're healthy).

The Four Fundamentals of Health

Being healthy is not objectively difficult or complicated. However, we like to make it seem that way because it helps us justify why we aren't healthy, lean, and strong. Plus, very few health-based businesses that sell products or services benefit when we distill health down to the fundamentals. So, put away the articles and videos on how to make the perfect acai quinoa spinach kale flaxseed avocado smoothie, optimizing your vitamin levels, or having the most perfect physique, and let's just focus on getting good at the basics—that's more than enough.

The four fundamentals of health are all you need to become quite healthy. These are: getting the right amount of sleep, staying hydrated, eating clean, and exercising.

The best approach is to be well-rounded in all areas instead of being great in some areas and neglecting the others. Having a healthy diet doesn't mean much if you sleep only five hours a night. Exercising eight days a week doesn't mean much if you eat junk food all day. All of the aspects of health are equally important and play different roles in contributing to your overall health. Therefore, you should give them equal effort.

GETTING GOOD SLEEP

Good sleep is critical to human life. Those who get it experience a world of energy, cognitive sharpness, and physical health, but those who don't can barely function properly.

You're Probably Sleep-Deprived

If you don't routinely get eight to nine hours of good-quality sleep a night, you are sleep-deprived. This section is first in the health chapter for a reason. If you don't get the sleep aspect of your health down, you may as well not go through with the rest of this book, as you probably won't have the energy or cognitive power to do so. The benefits of sleep—but more importantly, the negative repercussions of not getting enough sleep—are not to be underestimated.

The Effects of Good Sleep

If I were to describe sleep as the body's way of recovering and supporting the function of every aspect of your physical health, I don't think sleep researchers would disagree. Proper sleep aids in our muscle recovery, strengthens the immune system, keeps our cardiovascular system healthy, and keeps us energized.

Sleep also ensures that the brain works at optimal levels. Sleep is tied to strong brain functioning including productivity and concentration, creativity, information processing, and emotional control.

Without any of those benefits, being social is hardly possible. Social people have the ability to be social because they're energetic, confident, and creative. This is only possible if your body and brain are working in the way they were designed to, and this is impossible without proper sleep.

How to Get Good Sleep

Good sleep can be broadly defined as eight to nine hours of uninterrupted sleep. However, it's not just the duration but also the quality that is important.

Duration is rather simple and straightforward. It is eight to nine hours of sleep, period. Seven hours is pushing the borders of sleep deprivation, and six hours or less is pretty much unacceptable for your body.

Quality is where it becomes more complex, as there are various different factors that contribute to the overall quality of sleep. As a general rule, you want to sleep and wake up at the same time every day. The room you sleep in should be dark, quiet, and cool. You should limit the substances you put into your body that will affect your sleep including alcohol, marijuana, and caffeine. In the hours before you go to sleep, you should stop exposing yourself to blue light. Don't engage in any stressful activities like working or exercising.

STAYING HYDRATED

Getting enough water into your body is extremely important for optimal health.

Water makes up 60 percent of an adult's body. I like to say, "If something makes up 60 percent of your body, it better be important," and important it is. Water helps regulate body temperature, keeps joints lubricated, prevents infections, flushes waste out of your body through urine, delivers nutrients to cells, acts as the building block of new cells, and keeps organs functioning.

Take a look at the importance of water to your major organs and body parts:

- Your brain and heart are 73-percent water.
- Your lungs are 83-percent water.
- Your skin is 64-percent water.
- Your muscles and kidneys are 79-percent water.
- Your bones are 31-percent water.
- Your plasma (liquid portion of blood) is 90-percent water.

Being hydrated also improves sleep quality, cognition, and mood, which all directly contribute to confidence. It's safe to say that drinking enough water is vital to your health and confidence because your body is 60 percent of it, and your organs and overall health depend on it.

How to Stay Hydrated

Hydration is extremely simple. It's getting enough water into your body. The average adult male will need 3.7 liters of water a day; the average adult woman, 2.7 liters. About 20 percent of our recommended water intake comes from food, which means a man will need to drink about three liters of water a day, and a woman will need to drink between 2.1 and 2.2 liters.

Being hydrated also means limiting the number of drinks that dehydrate you, such as caffeine, alcohol, and sugary drinks. However, with proper hydration, these temptations and cravings should diminish greatly.

The closer you are to your water, the more likely you are to take sips when you feel the need. Carry a water bottle with you at all times or a glass when you're at home. If you get thirsty, it's too late. You should stay hydrated enough that you *don't* get thirsty.

If your goal is to drink three liters a day, measure how much water your bottle holds and track how many times you refill it. A standard plastic bottle is 500ml, which means you need to fill it six times during the day to get your recommended water intake (however, I recommend you use a reusable bottle instead). Four fills and a cup equal 2.2 liters.

Drink a cup or two of water after waking up to help your organs wake up, too, as they will be dehydrated as a result of you not drinking water during your sleeping hours. Room temperature or cool water at this time is best. Avoid cold water as this can shock the organs if consumed first thing in the morning. Dehydrating drinks such as coffee should not be your first drink in the morning.

Drink water during meals, as sugary drinks are the easiest way to add up unnecessary calories—or worse, sugar or aspartame.

HEALTHY EATING

You are what you eat. Food gives your human body the nutrients and energy it needs to function properly. All animals have a specific type of diet they must eat in order for their body to work properly, and humans are no different—although we have evolved to have a wider variety in our diet than many other animals.

The Modern Food Crisis

The world has become flooded with food that was never meant for us to eat. Companies have figured out how to manufacture "food" that is highly addictive and satisfies our taste cravings but is extremely unhealthy. And the consequence of flooding a society with extremely unhealthy, addictive, highly processed and additive-filled food is an extremely sick, overweight or obese, and unhealthy society—but the scariest thing of all is . . . this has become normal.

When you eat an unhealthy diet and tell your friends about it, they'll probably tell you about their own diets and how they're quite similar. It's not uncommon to eat junk food, consume sugary drinks and foods, eat lots of refined carbs, drink alcohol, not eat enough vegetables, eat too much meat, and go out to eat on a regular basis. But tell people that you eat a very clean, healthy, whole-foods diet, and you'll be met with envy, praise, and perhaps some negative remarks stemming from insecurity.

However, when an overwhelming majority of the population has the same diet problem, it is irresponsible, from a statistical standpoint, to blame all of them and chalk it up to laziness or indulgence without looking deeper into the factors.

Junk food, which includes processed foods, highly sugary or salty foods, or foods high in refined carbs, primarily comes from developed places where capitalism is the main economic engine. The reasoning behind this is simple: companies are incentivized to make as much money as possible; food is a big money market; real food such as crops and livestock are expensive to produce with little profit margin; and manufacturing, scientific, and engineering abilities exist. Add all of those together, and you get a company that is willing to engineer artificial food to make it as addictive as possible and keep people buying their products, therefore increasing their profit. Multiply this by thousands and thousands of companies, and you get a population that is flooded with toxic, highly addictive food that is designed to keep them craving it.

The formula for addicting humans to food is not a big secret. Humans naturally crave food that is salty, sugary, and fatty. If you make food that is high in carbs and low in protein, people can keep eating it without feeling full. Textures such as crunchiness in solids or fizziness in liquids also help to make products addicting. Add all of those together, and you get a typical potato chip that is very salty and fatty, high in carbs, and very crunchy. Or you get cookies or chocolate, highly sugary and fatty. Or you get a soft drink, which is fizzy and extremely sugary. These lab-designed foods can leave us quite powerless (both figuratively and literally) if we don't take an active role in keeping them out of our lives.

How to Eat Healthy

Implementing healthy eating comes down to the quality and quantity of food you eat.

Quality

Eat whole foods. It's that simple. Whole foods are plant- or meat-based foods that are unprocessed and unrefined, or processed and refined as little as possible before being consumed. Whole foods stay as close to their natural form as possible. Whole foods include whole grains, tubers, legumes, fruits, vegetables, and unprocessed meat.

Following this rule will help you to cut out all the highly processed foods that are loaded with refined grains, sugars, and additives. Highly processed foods are high in carbs, sugars, and fats, and have very little nutritional content. Even if they are fortified with nutrients, they cannot deliver the many healthy components of minimally processed foods. They lead to overeating and being overweight, lower energy and cognitive ability, and overall poor health due to less nutritional content. They also create long-term health problems.

Refined carbs (aka simple carbs or processed carbs) come in two forms: refined sugar such as table sugar (sucrose) and high-fructose corn syrup, and refined grains such as white flour. These types of carbs are stripped of almost all fiber, vitamins, and minerals. Refined carbs are digested quickly and have a high glycemic index. This means they lead to rapid spikes in blood sugar and insulin levels after meals. This can contribute to overeating, which is the goal behind many of these junk foods—remember, they're made by for-profit companies.

It's not overly difficult to maintain a healthy diet when you eat mostly whole foods, because everything you're eating is healthy and contains many of the nutrients you need. It's when you start shopping for those highly processed, food-like products that the confusion occurs, because you're bombarded by health claims and nutritional promotion.

When food products start claiming less sodium, less fat, more vitamins, and so on, the underlying assumption should be that these foods aren't healthy to begin with. If they were healthy, they wouldn't need to claim these things. It would be obvious. Apples and lean meat don't need to tell you they're healthy; they just are.

Like your mother used to tell you, make sure to eat your fruits and vegetables. Fruits and vegetables are absolutely loaded with nutrients that you wouldn't get elsewhere. These nutrients keep you in extremely good health in the short term and in the long term.

The short-term effects of eating fruits and vegetables include more energy, better mood, better sleep, and better memory—all traits you'll need to be successful socially. People today are eating too much meat, which is quite unhealthy. Eating fruits and vegetables has a front-end benefit of giving you the nutrients you need to be energetic, function properly, and be healthy, but it also has the back-end benefit of cutting out a lot of meat and other processed foods from your diet. I'm not telling you to become a vegan, but chances are, you are consuming too much meat and processed foods right now.

Removing processed foods from your house will make it a lot easier to be healthy. Making processed foods inaccessible to you in your house will make a huge impact in reducing your cravings because your brain will understand that it will take a great effort to obtain them.

It may help you to cook in bulk—you'll save time cooking individual meals. Your meals should have a good balance of whole grains, vegetables and fruits, and meat. It's useful to have a pack of spring greens or spinach and your favorite salad dressing on hand for an easy serving or two of vegetables.

Have healthy snacks around the house. Great options include fruits or yogurt with nuts.

It will help you tremendously to go to the grocery store with a list of things you want—that way, you won't shop impulsively.

Quantity

The average man needs to eat roughly two thousand five hundred calories a day; the average woman, two thousand.

If you eat a whole foods diet, this should be attainable for you, but as a general rule, don't eat until you're full. Eat until you're not hungry. Start using smaller plates, and get seconds if you need to instead of filling your giant plate and expecting to eat all of it.

Your daily calorie intake becomes a big problem when you violate the quality rule and start consuming processed foods. It's not uncommon for processed food meals to be over one thousand calories and innocent little snacks to be over five hundred calories. The average American eats three thousand six hundred calories a day, and you can bet the house that the majority of those calories are not coming from whole foods.

If you stick to the foods you were evolutionarily designed to eat, maintaining your health through food shouldn't be much of a problem.

PHYSICAL FITNESS

Being fit means three things: physical strength, cardiovascular health, and appropriate body mass index.

Physical Strength

Physical strength is developed through conditioning your muscles to lift heavy weights often. There is a balance here, as you want to develop muscle strength and endurance. Being able to lift heavy weights for many repetitions is more useful than being able to lift heavy but only a few times, so look to strike a balance between weight and repetitions.

The most effective way to gain physical strength and muscle mass is through heavy compound movements and consuming more healthy calories. Compound movements are movements that require multiple large muscle groups to work together. The opposite is isolation movements, where only one or a few smaller muscle groups work together. Building a strong body is difficult and takes too long when you stick to working one muscle group per exercise. Compound movements will hit many muscle groups at once, but just as importantly, they will strengthen the connective tissue and stabilizing muscles, which plays a vital role to overall strength. Think about a table: it doesn't matter how strong the wood pieces (major muscles) are, if the screws and glue (connective tissue and stabilizing muscles) cause the table to collapse.

- Do: Compound movements
    - Squats, dead lifts, rows, bench presses, overhead shoulder presses, dips, chin-ups, pull-ups
- Don't do: Isolation movements

- Bicep curls, triceps extensions, chest flys, hamstring curls, calf raises, leg extensions

I'm very far from being the gold standard of physical strength, but I'm also pretty far from being the scrawny weak boy I was before. The funny thing is that I've been working out at a gym since I was seventeen, but for the next three years or so, I saw little improvement in my strength and muscle mass. Now, I would say I'm above average in strength for my body weight. The difference between my early gym days and now is that I'm doing compound movements and have been progressively adding weight through a strength program. The funniest thing is that I was ignoring the part of the body mostly responsible for strength: legs. Squats and dead lifts might as well have been Arabic to me at that point because I didn't understand them. But now that I have packed on some muscle and strength, I am much more confident and happier than I was before.

Cardiovascular Health

Cardiovascular health is better developed through shorter periods of intensity over long-drawn-out cardio sessions. Fifteen to twenty minutes of intense cardio is better than an hour of light jogging, since the goal is to get your heart rate up. Like the balance of strength, you want to get your heart rate up but also be able to do so for a longer time.

As a general rule, if you can talk, watch a video, or play on your phone while you're doing your cardio exercise, it's too slow. Remember, your goal is to get your heart rate up for as long of a time as possible—it's kind of hard to talk or to scroll through Instagram when your heart is beating at 160 bpm.

Cardio has a reputation for being boring, but there are many ways to make cardio interesting, as there are many options. Cardio includes running, biking, rowing, boxing, swimming, sports, and jumping rope.

To me, running can be boring, but I can have a blast kickboxing the heavy bag. As a big mixed-martial-arts fan, I love studying striking martial arts such as Muay Thai and kickboxing, then practicing on the heavy bag. It's fun to learn, fun to do, and keeps me in terrific shape. Pick something you enjoy!

Weight Loss

Weight loss is another factor that greatly determines your physical health. It also affects your confidence, energy levels, self-esteem, and more.

Before we discuss weight loss, it's important that you get the four fundamentals of health right. The four fundamentals of health help ensure your body is working properly, and a properly working body is what is ultimately going to help you lose weight.

The goal with weight loss is not necessarily losing weight but losing fat. Although this may feel like the same thing on the surface, the more specific you can get, the better. Stepping on the scale and realizing you lost five pounds doesn't mean much if you can't identify how much fat you've lost. It could be water weight or muscle.

It's important to understand that nothing in the body happens by accident. Everything is controlled by your hormones.

How fast your heart beats, how much you urinate, and how happy you feel in this moment are all controlled by your hormones. Fat loss is no different. The main hormone to consider with fat loss is insulin.

Insulin is a fat-storing hormone. When you eat, your insulin rises, which signals to your body to store some of the food energy as fat. When you don't eat, your insulin falls, which signals to your body to burn some of the food energy—your fat. Higher-than-usual insulin levels tell our body to store more food energy as body fat. Tests have found that higher insulin levels cause you to gain fat.

Controlling your insulin levels requires you to change your diet. Controlling your insulin is composed of two factors—how high your insulin levels are after meals, and how long they persist. These two factors are dictated by what we eat and when we eat.

Historically, we were never *that* healthy in terms of the food we ate. The science of healthy food and exercise is only starting to reach the general public. Only in the seventies did fitness start becoming popular, and we weren't exactly eating all that healthy then either. Fast food, junk food, white bread, and sugary drinks were prevalent back then. Yet, the obesity rate started to rise significantly only in the eighties and continues to rise today.

Although you would be much better off eating healthy than not, there is one crucial difference between before the seventies and now: how often we eat. Three meals a day with some snacks in between used to be the social norm. Now, it's not uncommon for people to have five to six meals, plus snacks, during the day—nor is it uncommon for people to eat late at night.

Eating like this affects your body-fat levels, because when you eat, you store food energy as body fat, and when you don't eat (aka fast), you burn body fat for energy. If you eat three meals a day, your fat-storing and burning process is relatively balanced, which keeps fat levels regular. If you are eating constantly from the time you wake up to the time you sleep, the balance is completely off. There is no time for your body to burn fat, since the constant food intake is telling your body to store, store, store.

Let's use a bathtub as an analogy. Pretend your goal is to keep the bathtub as empty as possible but you have to fill it at certain points. If you turn on the tap and fill the tub with a gallon of water, then spend the next few hours slowly draining the water until the bathtub is empty (or close to empty), and repeat that process a few times a day, the bathtub will be fairly empty or completely empty by the day's end. But if you turn on the tap and fill the tub with a gallon of water, then leave the tap on all day, there's no way that the water will be able to drain to keep the bathtub empty. The same idea applies with constantly eating.

So, instead of eating five or six meals a day, cut down to three or so and stop eating snacks regularly in between. Consider intermittent fasting—the practice of time-restricted eating—and eat only during certain windows of time.

"If I stop eating all the time, won't I be hungry all the time?"

Not really. The feeling you get when you're hungry is just your body signaling to you to eat because it's not getting the food it's expecting at that time. The feeling of hunger is just a feeling, and if you don't give in to it, the feeling will eventually fade. Consider drinking a sugar-and-sweetener-free beverage during this time to cope with the urge. Keep in mind that the human body can go a month or more without eating—so you not eating for a few hours is not that big of a deal.

What Are You Stressed About?

When you're stressed, the stress hormone cortisol can increase your appetite for fatty or sugary foods. Stress can be both the cause and effect of weight gain.

Living with a partner with whom you are constantly arguing is one example of a stressful situation that can lead to overeating. The high levels of stress you'd experience in that situation could lead you to stress eat, and when we stress eat, it's usually high-calorie, fatty, sugary foods.

If you cannot address your sources of stress by yourself or aren't aware of what they are, it is recommended you talk to a professional therapist who specializes in stress to help you understand and overcome problems that cause you to overeat.

What Are You Trying to Escape From?

Food can create extreme feelings of pleasure that help us feel like we're escaping something. Similar to excessive alcohol and drug use, video-game playing, television watching, shopping, work, or exercise, people who are overweight may use food as an escape from an issue, whether that be a past trauma or current experience.

For example, if someone is at a job they can't stand, they may binge eat on the weekends and drink a lot to help them escape from the feelings that come from their job.

If you realize that a psychological issue is affecting your eating habits, you need to take the steps to solve it. Whether you take action yourself or talk to a professional, you must address the root of the problem. This is all a part of becoming healthier, and being healthy is critical to having energy, self-confidence, and motivation in social life and in life in general.

Health on Autopilot

When you build healthy habits, staying healthy becomes automatic and something you don't even need to think about. If you're constantly thinking about getting enough sleep, staying hydrated, eating clean, and working out, you may end up getting overwhelmed and failing.

There are two common mistakes people make when trying to build healthy habits. One, they try and set unrealistic expectations, and two, they try to take on too many things at once.

To find out if a habit is realistic or not, ask yourself if you can keep it up for the rest of your life. Going to the gym five times a week may be great when you're super motivated at the start, but that schedule is extremely difficult to keep up for a lifetime. Two to three times a week is more sustainable for most people.

When building habits, pick one thing to focus on and don't worry about anything else until it becomes automatic. Don't try to get good sleep, stay hydrated, eat clean, and get fit all at once. Pick one, make it automatic, then move on.

I put the four fundamentals of getting healthy in specific order, beginning with the most important.

1. Sleep
2. Hydration
3. Eating
4. Fitness

Each one of these four fundamentals serves as a foundation to take on the next one. Have you ever tried to work out when you're dehydrated and slept for five hours the night before? Wasn't pretty, was it? Let's take a deeper look.

1. Sleep: Without sleep, you will not have the energy to do anything else . . . Seriously a lack of sleep leads to stress, overeating, low energy, and low muscle recovery. Don't move on until your sleep is solid.
2. Hydration: Proper hydration will guarantee that your body and all its organs are working properly. Remember, most of your organs are well over fifty percent water. Brain, muscles, bones, and internal organs all need to be fully hydrated to function at optimal performance.
3. Eating: Food is going to give your body the right nutrition to be energized, but it doesn't have as big of an impact if you don't sleep or hydrate well, which is why it appears third on the list.
4. Fitness: Fitness is the last fundamental on the list. If you don't have all three previous fundamentals down, fitness can work against you, in a way. Low muscle recovery, added stress, low energy, and low nutrition when exercising can cause your body serious problems. But if you have all the other fundamentals down, becoming fit can absolutely change your world.

If You Hate Being Healthy, You're Doing It Wrong

If you move through the steps in this chapter correctly, getting healthy should be something you enjoy doing. To put it more bluntly, *if you hate being healthy, you're doing it wrong.* There are two things you should enjoy while becoming healthy: the actions themselves, and the results.

If the actions themselves are not enjoyable to you, figure out how to make them enjoyable, since you likely won't stick to anything for a long time if you don't like it. The actions I recommend in this chapter are not inherently unpleasant or difficult, but we make it seem like they are—especially if we have a lifetime of unhealthy habits we need to address. It may be difficult to give up excess amounts of junk food and fast food, but the meals you replace it with shouldn't be boring and bland; they should be just as tasty—only without all the sugar and sodium. You shouldn't be dragging yourself to the gym to workout, either. Becoming fit is almost impossible if you hate the process of lifting and doing cardio. With that being said, if your workouts consist of light weights and endless jogging, they may become boring and start to feel like a chore, though working out isn't inherently unpleasant. Could you push yourself to lift more? That would kick you out of boredom, since your mental energy would have to go towards lifting weight. Instead of jogging for an hour, how about a fifteen-minute session punching and kicking the heavy bag, or rowing? That would make cardio far more fun.

Even if you don't enjoy the action as much as you did when you started, the enjoyment you experience from the results should outweigh any sort of slight sacrifice you've made. I do admit that I would enjoy fast food and junk food more often if I could, but the result of being healthy—feeling energetic, mentally sharp, and in a consistent good mood—far outweigh any sort of marginal enjoyment I would get by increasing my unhealthy food intake. The feeling of waking up and being productive after a solid eight hours of sleep, the feeling of being energized from proper hydration, the feeling of being in a good mood from healthy food, and feeling good about and being in control of my body are feelings I wouldn't trade for anything, and I'm sure you'll feel the same way.

Self-Esteem through Style

The way you choose to present yourself to the world is going to dictate how the world presents itself to you. A big part of this is the way you dress. Although style is not related to health, it's in line with the benefits of optimizing your body. Being confident in your style is a big part of being confident in your appearance, which will make you feel better about yourself, give you more energy and motivation, and improve how others respond to you. Unlike health, style is highly subjective, and it would be extremely difficult to explain style through a book to a mass audience of varying genders, cultures, and personalities.

There are three general rules you should follow for finding the best style for you—the rest is a creative journey to find what you like. The first rule is to be intentional with your style. If you're wearing an outfit just because it was the only thing clean, you're doing it wrong. Aside from signaling to the world how they should treat you, you are also signaling to yourself how you should feel about yourself. Taking care of how you dress is going to inspire much more confidence and energy than throwing together a random outfit.

The second rule is to find what makes *you* feel good and confident. You might feel a temptation to buy the most expensive clothes that your favorite celebrity or fashion media source is promoting, but in most cases, you're better off finding the style that makes you feel good and confident. The most impactful change you can make today is to only wear clothes that fit. A well-fitting gray T-shirt might make someone feel way more confident than a thousand-dollar outfit.

The third rule is to make sure your grooming is superb. A well-groomed person signals confidence, conscientiousness, and care. Good grooming can make you significantly more confident and better looking.

Key Takeaways

- It's extremely difficult to be socially successful for a meaningful period of time if your body isn't working in the way it was meant to. Your body works in the way it's supposed to when you're healthy.
- Being healthy is not objectively difficult or complicated. If you follow the four fundamentals of health, it is a simple process.
- The four fundamentals of health are getting good sleep, staying hydrated, healthy eating, and physical fitness.
- By focusing on building healthy habits, your health will become virtually automatic and relatively effortless.
- If you're not enjoying being healthy, you're doing it wrong.
- The way you present yourself to the world through your style is going to dictate how the world presents itself to you.

CHAPTER 7

Feeling Comfortable, Feeling Positive

If there was a bomb in the park where you were relaxing and someone put a sign around it declaring it safe, or tried to convince you it wasn't going to go off, you likely wouldn't feel any better. The only way you would feel safe is if a bomb squad proved it was defused . . . or if you got the heck out of there.

Think back to the last time you were hanging out with someone who just seemed a little "off" to you. Maybe they were nervous and talking a little too fast. Maybe they didn't smile all that often, or maybe they seemed a bit too tense, like they were overthinking something negative. Perhaps their actions made you feel a bit uneasy. Chances are that when you were around this person, you didn't feel entirely comfortable. And chances are, you noticed a change in your own reactions. You might be an overall cheerful person, but around them, you might have become nervous too. Looking back now, do you think this person was successful in their social life?

The principle of this chapter is how to make other people feel comfortable and positive. The reason you need to make people feel comfortable and positive is because those are the two basic feelings one must have in order to feel safe. Safety is the most fundamental feeling one needs to have in order to enjoy their interactions with you. Our instincts are always assessing if someone might be a potential threat to us, especially if it's our first time meeting them. Making someone feel comfortable and positive in your presence is a great way to relieve some of those instinctual fears so that you can have an enjoyable interaction.

Think about it: Have you ever enjoyed a conversation in which you didn't feel positive? Have you ever had fun and let loose around people who didn't make you feel safe? Have you ever felt positive around someone who was obviously nervous and anxious? Of course not!

But *the key in making someone feel comfortable and positive around you is to make yourself feel comfortable and positive.* When doing so, you naturally project those feelings outward, which invites the other person to feel comfortable and positive too.

Feeling comfortable means you are comfortable enough with who you are to contribute to the interaction without negative feelings or discomfort potentially turning someone off.

Feeling positive means your internal state is positive enough to make your contributions to the interaction friendly and happy.

Unfortunately, many good, well-intentioned people fail at making others feel comfortable and positive because they themselves don't feel comfortable and positive. Whether it's because they're not socially skilled, they're socially anxious, or they're not in the present moment and thinking about something else, many people fail to make the people around them want to stick around.

Although feeling comfortable and positive is an entire psychological process in and of itself, there are two major factors that contribute to you feeling comfortable and positive. When you're involved in a social interaction with others, social anxiety stops you from feeling comfortable, since your mind is preoccupied with negative thoughts and emotions, and not valuing yourself prevents you from feeling positive, since you're not confident enough to express your true self and be vulnerable.

Solve Social Anxiety

Social anxiety stops many people from feeling comfortable in social situations. Social anxiety can come in the form of being too anxious to go outside, attend a social event, talk to a new person, have a conversation, stay attentive, etc.

Signs that you may have social anxiety include excessive self-consciousness in everyday social situations; intense worry for days, weeks, or months about an upcoming social situation; fear that you'll act in ways that will embarrass or humiliate yourself; fear that others will notice you're nervous; and/or being unwilling to engage in social situations.

Social anxiety can be quite a difficult thing to overcome. Doing so requires you to learn about your current fears, identify and challenge your current thoughts, reprogram your mind, address insecurities, and take steps to expose yourself to new experiences.

OVERCOME THE FEAR OF REJECTION

Fear of rejection happens when you're afraid of feeling ostracized by other people. Whether this takes the form of not talking to a new person, not saying what you want to say in a conversation, or not asking someone to meet up, fear of rejection stops you from expressing yourself authentically in social interactions.

There are many factors that can cause someone to reject you. Even if you're the coolest person in the world, you will still experience rejection. It may happen because of you, it may happen because of the other person, or it may happen because of something you have no control over. Trying to understand why you get rejected only works up to a certain extent, and most of the time you probably won't find out.

To try and blame all rejections on other people is foolish. Things that may cause people to reject you that are within your control include: your appearance, your social anxiety, the topics of conversation you bring up (or don't bring up), your lack of social skills, and any potential negative vibe that you may bring. In short, in some cases, any rejection that centers around you can most likely be improved by making others feel safer and better.

By a similar token, trying to blame all rejections on yourself is equally foolish. Blaming all rejections on yourself and assuming you're at the center of all rejections is an emotional reaction that clouds your response to something simple and logical. Interactions require two people at the very least.

When someone rejects you, it's entirely possible that it has nothing to do with you. If you have decent self-awareness, you should be able to detect when something was your fault versus when it wasn't. Rejection that's not your fault usually comes down to two things: someone else's insecurity and/or a situational problem. Oftentimes, you may not ever find out for sure.

People feeling insecure is extremely common. It is the most common cause of rejections that are not yours to blame. Sometimes, you'll either say or represent something, whether directly or indirectly, that makes whomever you're speaking with feel insecure. This can cause them to shut you out socially.

For example, if Maya, who is physically fit and good looking, walks into a room, and Sarah, who is overweight, is not comfortable in her own skin as a result of Maya's presence, Sarah may not want to talk to Maya, not because of anything Maya did wrong, but because she represents something that triggers Sarah's insecurity.

Sometimes, something that is neither your fault nor the fault of whomever you're in the presence of stops you from having a satisfying social interaction, even if you and that person or people may connect well on a separate occasion. Examples of this can include a coworker not wanting to talk to you because their boss is nearby, someone not wanting to talk to you because they're talking to someone they're interested in or attracted to, or because they have their mind on something else like work.

Although these situations are simple and logical, we still find ourselves taking them personally. It's natural to do that, but understand that rejections happen, and they're not always your wrongdoing.

Just knowing that rejections aren't always your fault may be a great relief to some and will hopefully help to reduce the fear of rejection tremendously.

Self-Esteem and the Fear of Rejection

The human brain works differently than what you're used to believing. You may believe that the human brain is rational—that its default is to objectively lay out all the facts and information of a situation in order to come to the best possible conclusion. While that is true for a very small percentage of our total thoughts, most of our thoughts are emotional. When our brain operates on emotions, it creates an emotional conclusion, and we find the facts or information that will confirm our preexisting verdict. This is called confirmation bias.

Inner security, self-confidence, self-esteem, whatever you wish to call it, is an emotional perception of yourself. Your emotional perception of yourself might be somewhere between "I completely suck and am worthless" to "I'm the greatest person in the world." For people who are terrified of rejection, it looks something like, "I'm not good enough for people, and I don't like myself."

When a person rejects you, they are sending you information. The information is that they do not want to talk to you for whatever reason. Rejection either confirms or conflicts with your preexisting emotional conclusion of yourself. If you're afraid of it, rejection confirms your preexisting conclusion: that you don't like yourself and you're not good enough. The opposite of this is when rejection conflicts with your preexisting emotional conclusion of yourself. Those with high, healthy self-esteem don't take rejection as poorly or personally, since they don't use rejection as validation for the fact that they dislike and don't accept themselves.

Self-Esteem Through Self-Acceptance

Once you learn how to accept yourself, you will fear the potential unacceptance of others much less. But there is a catch: you have to honestly accept and appreciate who you are. This is not something that you can fake, because the only person who benefits, and the only person who you're accountable to, is yourself.

Acceptance can feel like an abstract, new-age topic when we speak about it in terms of accepting ourselves, but it becomes extremely clear and simple to understand when we look at it through the lens of accepting who you are.

Think about a person you know personally whom you respect. Why do you respect them? You likely respect them because they respect themselves and are a respectable person. They take care of themselves, they are self-assured, they are humble, they are kind, they are honest, they are vulnerable and courageous, and they do things you admire. Self-acceptance isn't much different. Instead of respecting another person, you're respecting yourself.

There are two main sources of self-acceptance that you will need to address in order to learn how to respect yourself: being comfortable with the negative aspects of yourself and appreciating the positive aspects of yourself. Self-acceptance is a byproduct of doing these two things right.

The entire skills development part of this book is designed to help you recognize and create positive attributes within yourself. Here is a summary of how these skills help you accept who you are:

- Developing deep connections with those you care about brings meaning and fulfillment to your life.
- Meeting new people helps you to associate yourself with people that bring you joy and fulfillment.
- Vulnerability helps you to create opportunities that benefit your life.
- Health and fitness help you to be confident at the most basic, biological level.
- Feeling comfortable and positive helps you be in a good state of mind.
- Developing social skills helps you feel comfortable with your ability to communicate and belong in the world.
- Enjoying being alone helps you enjoy peace of mind with yourself.

This chapter is designed to help you address and become comfortable with the negative aspects of yourself that keep you from accepting yourself fully: fears, irrational thoughts, insecurities, and a lack of self-respect.

It's important to note that self-acceptance doesn't come when you finally "arrive" at a place where things are perfect. You can accept who you are now—even if you're still working on improving yourself. Self-acceptance and self-improvement are not mutually exclusive. Self-acceptance happens when you appreciate yourself *and* are comfortable with your perceived flaws and the prospect of being uncomfortable and failing.

Like a good parent or friend who loves and accepts you unconditionally, self-acceptance is ultimately the practice of loving and accepting yourself unconditionally.

Experience Rejection

Regardless of how much you mentally prepare and improve yourself to a place of self-acceptance, you're still going to get rejected in the real world, and this is precisely how you start to overcome it.

The more and more you experience rejection and deal with it in healthy ways, the more and more you realize that it's not such a big deal. For those who've experienced little rejection or have dealt with it in poor ways, the thought of rejection not being such a big deal seems almost unfathomable, but those who've experienced rejection and dealt with it well know exactly what I'm talking about. By dealing with rejection in healthy ways, we can use it to succeed in the future.

After I held multiple jobs where I cold-called companies all day, after I approached and asked out many women and practiced vulnerability for years, my fear of rejection dramatically diminished. This is not to say that I'm totally unafraid, but I'm able to act effectively despite the fear.

There are exceptions to this rule. Moments in which you are heavily emotionally invested or the rejection is particularly brutal are going to hurt, no matter how mentally healthy you are. But accepting that rejection is a part of life, and being willing to put yourself in situations where you may get rejected to serve a higher goal is the whole point of life. Life isn't lived cowering from rejection, but instead comes when you embrace it.

There are good ways to go about experiencing rejection, and there are poor ways to go about it. A good way is what we've outlined in this chapter: understand the nuances of rejection, and be aware and honest about it while developing high self-esteem through self-acceptance. Poor ways of experiencing rejection can include exclusively blaming one source for your rejections, whether that be yourself, others, or your circumstances, or flooding yourself with too much rejection without experiencing enough success.

We've outlined the logical reasons why rejection is sometimes your responsibility, sometimes the other person's fault, and sometimes the blame of neither (assuming that you're able to look at the rejection objectively). Unfortunately, because rejection is such an emotional process, looking at rejection emotionally is far too common. When you exclusively blame one source, there is often an underlying reason why. This can lead to anger, frustration, sadness, and hopelessness, if left unaddressed.

Flooding yourself with too much rejection without experiencing enough success is another poor way of handling rejection. This typically happens when you or someone else tells you that the best way to overcome your fear of rejection is to get rejected as much as you can, so you realize it's not a big deal. While that is theoretically true to an extent, in practice it is a disaster. There is nothing noble about getting rejected. No success or wisdom comes as a result of getting rejected if you don't also see success in the process—it can lead to bitterness and lack of motivation. Each rejection should serve as a learning opportunity to get you closer to success. Rejection in itself isn't anything you need to "get used to."

IDENTITY AND CHALLENGE BELIEFS

Throughout your everyday life, you'll constantly be exposed to all types of thoughts—positive and negative. The problem is that if you're insecure, sad, and lonely, these negative thoughts are going to be quite common.

The good news is you can learn to manage them. Learning to manage your thoughts will help you keep a clearer state of mind, but actual improvement in your life is also required to bring you there. If your brain is in a constant state of sadness, insecurity, and loneliness, it has very good reasons to flood you with negative thoughts. The key is to work on both the internal and external aspects of your improvement as they will complement each other nicely.

Mindfulness

Mindfulness means to focus on being aware in the present moment while calmly accepting your thoughts, feelings, and bodily sensations. Mindfulness helps you keep a calm state of mind, as you are not occupying your mind with anything other than the present moment.

The key concept in mindfulness is accepting your thoughts and feelings without judgement. You accept your thoughts and feelings for what they are: thoughts and feelings. You don't judge them or yourself for having them, and you don't unintentionally engage in them.

This is a powerful tool because the sooner you realize that your thoughts and feelings are not you, you stop getting controlled by them as easily. If Jessica is sitting in her room after work watching *Grey's Anatomy* and a thought pops into her mind that tells her she's annoying and no one likes her, if she isn't being mindful and doesn't understand that her thoughts and feelings are not who she is, she may subconsciously engage in the thought and start going down a negative rabbit hole, which can throw off her mood for the rest of the night. However, if she is being mindful, she can accept her thoughts for what they are—just thoughts and not reality—without judging herself or the thoughts.

Mindfulness is a constant practice. The better you get, the less conscious effort you'll have to put into it—just like any habit.

Many people have experienced tremendous mindfulness benefits through meditation. Mindfulness meditation is the conscious practice of staying present, although you don't have to meditate to be mindful.

While mindfulness is a fantastic practice that will help you disengage many of the negative thoughts you feel throughout your day, there are still going to be certain thoughts that dominate your thinking, and being mindful may not help to effectively deal with them, unless you pair it with a constant practice and the following healthy habits.

Challenging the Validity

Many of the negative thoughts that can come to dominate your mental bandwidth aren't even valid. Chances are, you have multiple thoughts that dominate your mind, but have you ever taken the time to think through whether or not they are valid, or did you assume that if it pops up in your mind, it's legitimate?

The goal of challenging validity is to create a reason based on logic, so you can appropriately deal with your thoughts. If you realize the logic doesn't make sense, then you can work to be mindful of it, since you've discovered the holes in your argument. If the logic does make sense, then you work to address the thought in the most appropriate way.

Since most negative thoughts come in the form of a problem, let's challenge the validity of those thoughts by asking the following questions:

- What do you think is the problem?
- Why is it a problem for you? (Keep asking yourself why here. You may realize you don't actually have a good reason. Problem solved. Sometimes, the conscious awareness of your reasoning is enough to eliminate the problem.)
- What do you think is causing the problem?
- How does it make you feel?
- Is there external evidence that this is a problem?
- What would be the worst thing that could happen?
- What is likely to happen?
- What can you do to solve the problem?

A FEW EXAMPLES

Valid problem: Melissa is too nervous to go out because she's shy.

- What do you think is the problem?
    - She's too shy to go out and meet new people.
- Why is this a problem?
    - Because she feels like people won't like her.
- What do you think is causing this problem?
    - Inability to hold fun and interesting conversations.
- How does this make you feel?
    - Sad and alone, since she doesn't have any friends and can't seem to make any.

- Is there any external evidence that this is a problem?
    - She can think about instances where conversations stalled out or just ended in an awkward silence.
    - Maybe she realizes it's just a feeling she has instead of an actual problem. It's self-perception more than a reality-based issue.
    - Maybe she realizes her problem isn't about her conversation skills but instead about making people feel comfortable in conversation.
- What would be the worst thing that could happen if Melissa goes out to meet new people?
    - This depends on Melissa's creativity (or paranoia), but the worst thing that could probably happen is that she gets rejected by someone when she tries to talk to them, and everyone laughs at her as she runs out of the room in tears.
        - The point of this exercise is to put into words the worst thing that could happen, so you get a real, clear image instead of some vague sense of fear. Of course, this would be terrible if it were to happen, which is the point, but the odds of this happening are extremely small (unless Melissa is walking into a room of insecure raging jerks).
- What is likely to happen?
    - She goes out and either stands around awkwardly or starts talking to a new person in either an awkward or fun conversation.
- What can she do to solve this problem?
    - She can learn conversation skills.

    - She can focus on becoming more comfortable in social situations.

Invalid problem: Derek thinks everyone will hate him if he goes out and meets people.

- What do you think is the problem?
    - Derek thinks that he is unlikeable, and everyone will hate him if he tries to meet new people.
- Why is this a problem?
    - Because if he goes out and gets rejected, he will feel sad and dislike himself.
- What do you think is causing this problem?
    - His own low self-image.
- Is there any external evidence of this being a problem?
    - No, actually, a lot of people think he's a pretty cool man. He has friends already.
        - Sometimes you may think something is a problem until you go through the steps and try to find evidence for it.

Challenging your own negative thoughts is likely to clarify flaws in certain thoughts that you may have. Now that we've established what's real and legitimate, we can focus on addressing the actual insecurities.

ADDRESSING INSECURITIES

Even if you're working on understanding rejection and accepting yourself and are practicing mindfulness and challenging the validity of your irrational thoughts, you are still going to experience negative thoughts and emotions. The good news is that through this process, the causes of those thoughts and emotions are going to be real problems. The bad news is that the thoughts and emotions come from real problems. The good news is that insecurities can be addressed. The bad news is that it can be difficult, or you can only improve them to certain extents.

Insecurities come in all different forms. Insecurities can be physical such as your appearance, height, hair, acne, asymmetries, or body shape. They can be social such as your conversational abilities, shyness, or intelligence. They can also be emotional such as jealousy, your emotional state, need for validation, trust issues, or feelings of inadequacy. All are valid.

The ultimate goal with addressing insecurities is to accept yourself. You don't need to become a perfect human and be flawless physically, socially, and emotionally. The goal is to get you to a point where you are comfortable with and appreciate yourself. By that same token, not all insecurities need to be solved. The ones that you should address are the ones you identify as holding you back from accepting yourself, the ones that stop you from being comfortable with yourself in social situations.

When you identify an insecurity you'd like to address, you can choose to address the cause or the emotional reaction. The strategy will depend on the specific insecurity, and while it's best to address both, in some situations you may be able to address only the emotional reaction.

During my first year of undergrad, I developed terrible acne on my face and upper body, which caused me to be extremely shy and insecure. Although I spent a lot of time working on my emotional reaction to it, it was clear I needed to tackle the cause in order to feel secure. Through a year of doctor's trips and advanced medication, I was able to solve it.

For some insecurities, dealing with your emotional reaction is all you need to do, or all you can do. If you get extremely jealous when your best friend is better friends with someone else, you can try to make them better friends with you if you think that's a good idea. However, working on your emotional reaction would be a healthier solution.

Addressing the Cause

The first step to addressing the cause of your insecurity is to understand your emotions. How does this insecurity make you feel? When you ask yourself this question, refuse to answer it in a fluffy or dismissive way, because if you felt only kind of sort of bad about it, it wouldn't be an insecurity in the first place. You need to develop a healthy but burning desire to overcome your insecurities if you are actually going to do so, or else you'll never have the motivation to overcome them, because insecurities can be difficult to manage.

The next step is to educate yourself on the topic, how it affects you, how you can overcome it, and how others have overcome it. There is virtually no insecurity that you can experience that many other people haven't had and overcome already. But you need to become very knowledgeable on all aspects of your insecurity if you want to have the logical understanding of how to get through it. Lucky for you, pretty much everything you need to know exists on the internet.

Last but not least, you need to devise a legitimate course of action on how you'll solve it. The best place to start is to look at the strategies other people have employed and adopt those.

Bonus tip: Be accountable to yourself and to other people. Of course, you need to be disciplined towards yourself (with kindness to self) in order to follow through on your course of action, because nobody else but you is going to have 24/7 access to your progress. But you should also share your plan with a trusted person. That way, you'll have a social contract, which is a powerful biological tactic to keep you honest.

Addressing the Emotional Reaction

Insecurities cause an emotional reaction. In many cases, addressing the cause of the insecurity can help eliminate the insecurity, but in many other cases, you will have to deal with the emotional reaction.

Accept the Thought

The first step to addressing an emotional reaction to an insecurity is to accept it for what it is and how it makes you feel. The opposite of this is to avoid thinking about it, deny it, distract yourself, or suppress the thought.

If you are willing to admit your insecurity and take an honest look at yourself, you have taken an extremely difficult but important first step, and you are to be rewarded for that. Seriously, it's not uncommon for people to go long periods of time avoiding the truth.

Question Why You Feel This Way

Now that you admit the truth about how you feel, you should question why you feel this way.

Since insecurities are internal thoughts, it's worth asking: What does this insecurity say about me?

If you were courageous enough to be honest about how you feel, I hope you will be courageous enough to investigate why you feel this way and what it says about you.

An emotional man could come to the conclusion that he beats himself up for not having the ability to be socially savvy. A short man could discover that he feels inferior to taller men. An overweight woman could realize that she is uncomfortable with other women getting more attention from men than her.

If, at this point, they discover that their emotional reaction can be solved by addressing the cause, they should take the steps outlined previously.

Practice Compassion to Self

Compassion to self is treating yourself how a best friend would treat you. A best friend doesn't beat you up, emotionally abuse you, and disrespect you. Instead, they support you, cheer you up, and accept you while being honest with you and keeping you accountable. From now on, your brain is your best friend. This will make being compassionate to yourself much easier, since your brain won't be actively working against your comfort and confidence.

Comparison and perfectionism are two common thought patterns that work against your ability to have compassion to self. When you compare yourself to others, you prevent yourself from focusing on yourself, since your metrics are no longer internal, but instead relative to another person. The danger of comparing yourself to somebody is that you can always find a way to feel good about yourself by thinking of someone you're "better" than, and you can always find a way to feel bad about yourself by thinking of someone you're "lesser" than.

Perfectionism is similar to comparison as it stops you from being compassionate towards who you are currently. Unlike comparison, where you're measuring yourself against someone, perfectionism is when you compare yourself to the image of perfection you have, and every flaw you perceive serves as a harsh critique to your lofty, unrealistic expectations.

If you find yourself comparing yourself to others or being a perfectionist, it's worth going back and questioning why you feel this way. You need a clear picture of what is causing you to try and achieve standards that don't come from a good place.

It's worth finding affirmations that make you feel compassionate toward yourself and repeating them until the thought process becomes a mental habit. If you think affirmations are goofy and strange, that's the entire point. It's supposed to feel goofy and strange at first, since your words and your mind are not yet in line, but fully commit to it anyway.

Affirmations are like a good parent teaching their young child to stop crying and stand up straight. The child might scream and cry in the moment, but it's up to the parent to make them act in a certain way. As the parent continues to instill this behavior into the child and the child grows up and learns more about life, they start realizing that not crying and standing up straight helps them navigate the world better. They start not crying and standing up straight without the parent telling them to do it, because they know that this serves them better.

Great self-affirmations include:

- "Even though I'm feeling ____, I love and accept myself anyway."
- "I accept the best and worst aspects of who I am."
- "Changing is never easy, but it's easier if I stop being hard on myself."
- "I deserve kindness, love, and empathy from myself."
- "I don't need to be better than ____; I need to be better than who I was yesterday."
- "I don't need to be perfect; I just need to do my best."
- "I will be patient and trust the process."

FOCUS ON THE INTERACTION

Social anxiety happens when you're focused on yourself. When you're focused on yourself, especially when you're focused on the negative aspects, thoughts like, "Does this person like me?" or, "Did I say something stupid?" pop into your head and can derail the opportunity to have a great interaction.

Instead of worrying about yourself, develop the habit of focusing on the interaction. When you do this, you focus on fun. You're able to talk about interesting things, get to know the other person, and enjoy yourself without being distracted by the internal, self-conscious dialogue.

DEALING WITH THE PHYSICAL SYMPTOMS OF SOCIAL ANXIETY

It's not uncommon to be nervous, become shaky, have difficulty talking, and start blushing when you're socially anxious. Even if you have dealt with the emotional and mental aspects of social anxiety, you still may have physical symptoms when you're in social situations.

When this happens, start to calm yourself down by focusing on your breathing. Slow, calm breathing will help calm your mind and body and bring it back to a more grounded state. From there, you can assess whether or not you have the ability to perform the task at hand.

If the task seems manageable and doable, it's up to you to have the courage to do it. The good thing is that confidence comes from repeated successful performance, so if you are able to do whatever task is making you nervous now, even if you don't do it well, you are well on your way to developing real confidence.

If the task seems overwhelming and almost impossible to you, it is worth starting out slow and taking progressive steps instead of trying to do everything all at once. If you're afraid of attending big group events, you can start out by talking to people in comfortable situations, then moving to one-on-one meetups, then working your way up to group events. How do you eat an elephant? One bite at a time.

Respect Yourself

When you respect yourself, you value yourself highly enough to start expressing yourself truthfully. This will help you to become happier with yourself. Respecting yourself is also a key part in feeling positive in social situations, since other people tend to respect you to the extent that you respect yourself. Respect comes from appreciating the perception of high value somebody has. Everyone whom you respect comes as a result of you perceiving them to have high value, and everyone who respects you comes as a result of them perceiving you to have high value. Other people's perception of your value comes from your perception of your own value.

A caveat to valuing yourself is that it has to be authentic. Pretending to value yourself by acting or overcompensating will almost always fail, because people's social instincts are very alert to even the subtlest behavioral cues.

The good news is that feeling comfortable with yourself by working through social anxiety is a big part of the battle. By properly working through social anxiety, you will eliminate many of the things that would otherwise cause you to diminish your own value. This section is dedicated to actions you can take to practice valuing yourself.

PERSONAL CONGRUENCE

Personal congruence is when you're consistent with your personality throughout all your social situations and you talk and behave in line with your true desires and intentions. This is the definition of being yourself and is only achievable through a commitment to your authenticity.

The reason why personal congruence commands respect is because it is a signal of rock-solid internal security. People who are personally congruent see no reason to change their personality to please others and are confident enough with themselves to act in a way that reflects their true desires.

Personal congruence also commands respect from others because it commands trust from others. Distrust comes when you suspect that someone isn't being entirely truthful, has ulterior motives, or when they act in different ways around different people. A personally congruent person blows any sense of distrust out of the water through pure authenticity.

Personal congruence will allow you to be the best and most enjoyable version of yourself because you won't have to put on a fake persona to fit into a social situation or to impress others. You won't need to seek validation from others, as you're comfortable with getting the validation that comes from people appreciating the real you. And you will act in a way that you want, which means you will be free from the sense of needing recognition.

The beautiful thing about being personally congruent is that the people who gravitate towards you end up really liking you. You gain that mass liking for a very counterintuitive reason—because you're openly inviting people to dislike you. When you are completely and unapologetically yourself, you are putting your true self on display and subconsciously telling people to take it or leave it. The ones who aren't so thrilled with you slowly back off and disappear from your life, but the ones that like you voluntarily keep paying attention and voluntarily stay a part of your life, often resulting in them liking you more. As a result, the ones who do end up staying are there because they like you and want to be there. It doesn't feel forced because it's not.

Deny the Burning Need to be Validated

In order to become free to act in the way that is congruent with who you are, you will need to overcome the need for validation. This becomes possible when you deny the desire for recognition.

Seeking validation will mentally trap you into living to satisfy the needs of others. If you catch yourself saying things to yourself like, "I will do this if I get recognized and appreciated for it," or "It's not worth doing this if I don't get recognized and appreciated for it," you are treating your behavior as a means to get validation or acceptance, which means you're not being yourself.

If you do anything that does allow you to be greatly recognized, such as posting on social media, giving a presentation to a crowd, or receiving an award, make sure you are doing those things for the purpose of doing them, and don't have any expectations for recognition. The last part is especially important.

Practice Being Blunt

Bluntness is when you are clear and truthful in what you say, without any filters or indirection. This should not be mistaken for being rude or malicious. Bluntness is saying what you mean.

When you practice bluntness, you'll stop altering your own personality to please others. This will give you a new sense of social freedom that you probably never would have been able to achieve if you constantly tried to censor your speech.

It's easy to be blunt when you're telling someone what they want to hear, but the real freedom comes when you start telling people what they *don't* want to hear, but what you consider to be objectively true. Once again, it has nothing to do with being rude or malicious—it's about not covering up your true intentions or desires with a veil of pleasant speaking. It's fine if you need to add certain phrases to make others more receptive to your message, as long as you don't cover up your true intention.

If you want to express your discontent, you can say, "I didn't like this."

- Examples of *not* being blunt in this situation include giving a fake compliment or saying something was okay when in reality you did not like it. Just say you didn't like it. Not everything has to be great, and if it isn't good and you tell the person in a non-malicious way, they can take the feedback and improve.

If you want to say no to something, you can say, "No, thank you," or just, "I'm good."

- Examples of *not* being blunt in this situation include saying yes when you actually don't want to and making up an excuse. Just say no. Be considerate when you say no, but don't sacrifice your own desires to spare someone else the pain of rejection.

If you want to ask for something, you can say, "Hi, can I get ___ from you?" or "Can you do ___ for me?"

- Examples of *not* being blunt in this situation include giving signals that you need help or creating covert social contracts. Just act directly; you're far more likely to get what you want.

One thing that holds a lot of people back from practicing bluntness is the fear or guilt of other people's negative reactions. Simply put, you're not responsible for other people's emotions. The only exception is if your intention is to hurt someone else. But if you are blunt with no ill intention, you are not responsible for how the other person reacts.

Live Up to Your Core Values, and Don't Compromise Them

A sign of a strong, respectable person is that they have values and they don't compromise them. Values make up who you are. Your ability to uphold good values demonstrates integrity, clarity of purpose, and self-respect.

What You Do Is What You Are

Values are not about what you say, but instead about what you do. How you behave and what actions you take determine your values. Your words communicate your behavior. If you ever want to take a hard look at yourself, don't look at the words you say, but look at what you've consistently done—your actions.

One can say they value something, but if their actions say otherwise, then they don't truly value what they say they do. However, if they change their behavior once they become aware of a more important value, then this is proof that they truly value it. It's all about behavior.

The giant oil corporation who claims to "be committed to the responsible treatment of our environment" but pays employees low wages to dispose of toxic waste in a lake clearly values money and taking shortcuts over their supposed value of "commitment to environmental responsibility."

But values can also be a lot subtler and not very obvious. The workaholic who spends 80 hours a week in the office may be looked at as a person who values making a positive impact on society and providing for their family. However, if you dig deeper and realize the reason why they spend eighty hours a week in the office is so they can avoid fixing the problems with their spouse, it may become apparent they don't value working as much as they value hiding from problems.

Hold On Tight

Everyone wants to make a lot of money, everyone wants to be honest, everyone wants to have friends, everyone wants to be ethical, everyone wants to be healthy, but the strength of your values lies in what you prioritize over others. In our world of abundance, the word *prioritization* seems to get lost.

Values are about prioritization. When push comes to shove, which one do you choose over the other? You can't prioritize your health *and* your work; you have to prioritize your health *over* your work. You can't prioritize a night of *Call of Duty* with your friends *and* being social; you have to prioritize a night of *Call of Duty* with your friends *over* being social (hopefully not in that order, but that's up to you).

Prioritization may not be much of a problem in your everyday life where conflicts or tough decisions don't happen constantly, but sometimes, your values get pressure tested when you're forced to make a difficult decision. This is when you double down and strengthen your grip on your values.

The degree to which you sacrifice your values is the degree to which you disrespect yourself and therefore allow others to disrespect you, as you are not congruent with what you believe.

Having values but giving them up when the going gets tough signifies one of two things. You either don't have the ability to uphold values that are important to you, or you are willing to compromise your values. Both will likely cause you to lose respect for yourself and others.

SET AND ENFORCE STRONG BOUNDARIES

Boundaries are the limits we set with ourselves and with other people. It's when we draw the line between what we will do and what we won't do, what we will tolerate and what we won't tolerate. Boundaries are the gateway to becoming respectable. When you have strong and healthy boundaries, you show people how they should act around you and how they should handle interactions with you.

Boundaries are important to a strong sense of respect because you are constantly choosing how other people treat you. Yes, you read that correctly. *You* are *constantly choosing* to let people treat you in the manner that they do.

Figure Out What Your Boundaries Are

Most of your boundaries are influenced by your overarching values. If your values include traits such as respect, responsibility, integrity, and honesty, then your boundaries in most situations are going to incorporate those.

With that being said, in situations where you find yourself often, such as at work, with friends, dating, and so on, it is definitely worth being conscious of what your boundaries are, so when you notice they're getting pushed, you will recognize it and be able to have an appropriate response.

If all else fails and you haven't had a chance to become fully, consciously aware of your boundaries, go with your gut and what feels right, as long as it's in line with your values.

Figure Out How to Enforce Your Boundaries

Most situations in which you need to enforce your boundaries will require you to use your words. However, there are situations where actions alone work, too.

The important thing to do when you are enforcing your boundary is to be direct, serious, and clear. Enforcing a boundary is not a regular interaction with another person. You enforce boundaries when something is becoming a problem, so the seriousness of the situation must be taken into consideration. You also need to be direct and clear to get your point across. The last thing you want to do is be overly friendly or overexplain your situation, as these are clear signals that you are not able to control yourself when you need to be serious. Pretend like you're a good, strong police officer. If you get stopped by one of those officers, they aren't going to be overly thrilled to talk to you, and they will make themselves clear.

When communicating your boundary, it's optimal to do these three things: explain your boundary, explain why it's important to you and why it affects you, and explain how you would like the other person to behave.

Explaining your boundary is simple, but this is where you need to be clear and direct. You need to let the other person know why this is important to you and/or how it affects you as they might not be sure, even if it seems obvious from your point of view. Lastly, you must communicate how you would like the other person to behave, as this will give them clear guidelines on how to move forward. When you do let somebody know how to behave toward you, set them up for success so that they're more likely to follow through with consistency.

Enforcing boundaries, especially if one is inexperienced or emotional about it, can turn into a messy situation. You always want to be calm and rational when you enforce a boundary. When you do enforce a boundary, be considerate of the other person, their point of view, and their feelings, too. You can't run around acting like a tyrannical dictator unless you want to lose another world war.

If things get emotional, do not attack the other person's character. The only thing you want to criticize is their behavior and its effects, not who they are as a person. If you want a guaranteed way to make sure somebody doesn't follow your boundary and maybe even actively goes against it, attack their character.

Keep your boundaries "I" centered, not "you" centered. Use phrases like, "I feel," "I would prefer the situation to be," etc. Using the word *you* will run the risk of hurting the other person's pride, causing them to be emotional.

Discuss any problems that the other person might have about your boundary or offer to elaborate on your boundary after they've responded. You want to make sure that all is resolved right there on the spot. If the person with whom you're speaking expresses any anger that you deem unreasonable, manage it and divert the focus back to being rational.

Here are some examples of strong and healthy versus poor boundary enforcement:

- They insult you.
    - Poor: "Hey, you idiot, don't call me a (insert insult)."
    - Poor: *Closes down and avoids confrontation.*
    - Strong and healthy: "Brad, I don't like being called a (insert insult). Please do not insult me ever again."

- They constantly complain around you.
    - Poor: "Shut up, stop being such a whiner."
    - Poor: "Aww it's okay. Yeah, this situation sucks." Or, "Tell me more."
    - Strong and healthy: "Look, I don't think you should be complaining about this situation this much, if it's not helping. When you're ready, you might want to look into some solutions that you can take to make this better."

Common boundaries that everyone should have:

- Saying no
- Not apologizing if you've done nothing wrong
- Not letting others insult you
- Speaking your mind openly
- Not explaining yourself all the time
- Not taking responsibility for other people's actions or emotions
- Calling out dishonesty or disingenuousness
- Not tolerating a weak, complaining, or victim mentality
- Not tolerating inconsiderate or rude behavior
- Not being friends with people you don't want to be friends with
- Not letting others interrupt you
- Protecting your personal free time
- Protecting your attention
- Protecting your personal space
- Protecting your money and resources

FEEL YOUR FEELINGS FREELY

Respectable people know how to manage their feelings. Respectable people are often seen as being cheerful and optimistic. This is no coincidence. They're not born with a special gift that you can't have; they're like this because they know how to manage their feelings, which enable them to feel positive emotions quite often.

The real test of how much you get to enjoy positive emotions is how well you can manage your negative ones. People who are unskilled at managing negative emotions typically do one of two things: express their emotions in unhealthy ways (lashing out, being narcissistic), or suppress their emotions. The problem with suppressing emotions is if you suppress one emotion, you suppress them all. Emotions are not like toppings on a pizza. You can't just throw away the ones you don't want; you have to take it all or take none of it.

More accurately, the degree to which you suppress one emotion is the degree you suppress all of them. When respectable people feel sad, angry, frustrated, jealous, and so on, they don't hide to themselves that they feel this way—they feel what they feel and deal with it effectively.

- Respectable people manage jealousy through appreciation.
- Respectable people manage hate through communication, forgiveness, and perspective.
- Respectable people manage sadness through compassion for self and rational thought.
- Respectable people manage frustration through consciousness and direction.

The people who are capable of feeling love and are able to express it freely are the ones who have a healthy relationship with all of their emotions. This leads them to a life of experiencing joy, laughter, happiness, and excitement—and all of the negative emotions, too.

Random Appreciation Stories

I've learned to give love freely to people in my life, without any reason or expectation at all. The reason why I express appreciation for people is because I feel like it. I have no ulterior motive, nor do I expect anything in return. This has made my life significantly better and has dramatically improved my relationships with people in my life.

The following examples aren't meant to be super amazing, life-changing stories, but instead are small yet meaningful bits of feeling my feelings freely from which you can take inspiration. The thing is, you don't need to be over-the-top when you experience your feelings freely. Most of the time, feeling your feelings freely is going to come from the minuscule, spontaneous moments of your life.

CEO Appreciation

When I was working at my first company, a new but fast-growing local startup, I got to witness firsthand what a good CEO looked like. By no means was this a Fortune-500 CEO, but it was definitely a person who was taking his company to good places.

I learned a lot, not only from observing him and the company but from studying business on my own time. I noticed he was doing a lot of things right, from how he organized his company to how he operated it.

However, it wasn't until half a year or so after I left that I fully realized what he was doing and how he was doing it. I started working at another local startup where I got a different perspective and started understanding business better. At that moment, I was inspired to send my former CEO a message letting him know what I realized.

I don't exactly remember what I sent specifically, but it was pretty much about how I thought he was doing a great job as a CEO and how I admired his work ethic, his level of thought, and how he carried himself. I thought he needed some words of encouragement, since his business was going through a rocky time, and I'm sure he didn't always get the reassurance.

I had no ulterior motive for sending the note. This wasn't me "building my network" or whatever self-centered professionals would say in that case. Just sincere appreciation.

Paying My Respects

The neighbors in the house I grew up in were amazing people who made my childhood significantly more memorable. Through chatting with me, doing favors for our family, or hosting us at their house for the annual New Year's event, they were great people and very much loved by our family. The father of the family, "Michael," was also an exceptionally talented handyman and saved our family from a number of expenses. He fixed our furnace, ventilation, dishwasher, and faucet without asking for anything in return. The family moved away when I was a teenager, and I have lost touch with them since, although there is no doubt we will always have a strong remembrance of one another.

One day, a few posts started popping up on my Facebook feed informing me that Michael passed away from leukemia. This made my heart sink. I hadn't been in touch with the family for so long, and this news seemingly came out of nowhere. After the initial shock, my mind immediately turned to his wife, "Lisa." I couldn't imagine what she was going through. Lisa had been so good to us during our childhood; the least I could do was reach out and extend my condolences.

We exchanged a few messages. I expressed how sorry I was for her loss, let her know how much Michael meant to us, and wished for her strength during these tough times. After we ended our conversation, I felt like I needed to do more. Then I remembered one time when I was younger and brought Lisa a gift back from Japan. It was a small hanging scroll decoration with Japanese art on it. I remember her cherishing the gift for a long time after. So, I decided to do something similar—I hopped on the internet and looked for a similar decoration, this time relating to the loss of a loved one.

I found an elegant piece with a lovely quote on it and promptly sent it to her. A week or so later, I got a very long emotional message from Lisa telling me the gift brought tears to her eyes and expressing her deep gratitude.

The quote read: "Those we love don't leave us; they walk beside us every day."

Everybody Needs a Therapist

I believe everyone needs a therapist. Not because everyone is mentally ill, but because everyone needs to be mentally healthy.

Therapy is a catchall term for psychiatrists, psychologists, counselors, and other social workers. Each of them has their own specializations. I personally have experience with psychologists and counselors, and I can tell you they can help address many problems that revolve around insecurities, anxiety, boundaries, and more.

Therapists are like doctors for the mind. In the same way you would go to the doctor if you had tightness in your chest or a broken toe, you would go to a therapist if you are feeling mentally stressed, anxious, depressed, and/or are dealing with a problem you don't have the specialization to fix. It doesn't necessarily have to be a severe mental problem for you to get a beneficial experience from a therapist. You don't only go to doctors when you're in serious pain or on the verge of death; you also go for checkups or minor issues. The same applies for therapists. Everyone needs to talk to a therapist, not because we all have crippling mental problems, but because we all need to be mentally healthy and address even seemingly small problems that can compound into bigger problems if left unchecked.

In modern culture, going to therapy still carries a stigma, although it's getting better. There are generally three reasons why someone is reluctant to go to a therapist.

The first is a general reluctance to get help. These are the people who prefer to tough it out or handle things on their own. Although they may justify their behavior by them being independent or strong, this is almost always a lie. It's an ego issue, and these people are unfortunately extremely lacking in self-awareness.

The second issue has to do with therapists specifically. Maybe someone is willing to go to a doctor but isn't willing to go to a therapist. This likely has to do with either the fact that mental health is not easily visible, as opposed to a flu or a broken rib, or they have some specific issue with therapists.

The third reason is they feel shame. They feel shame admitting that they have problems with their mental health and shame that they need to see someone to get those problems resolved. Feeling this way is normal; just don't let it get in your way. It takes courage to go to a therapist, but I can guarantee that every person who's done so will tell you how great of an experience it's been, and the people who talk negatively about it are usually the people who've never gone in the first place.

The more you think you don't need therapy, the more you need to go. If I'm being honest with you, if you've read this far, I highly recommend you visit a therapist. It may not seem obvious to you, but from someone with a nonemotional view, it makes sense. No one reads this book for fun. We've already covered the reasons why people typically don't feel comfortable and positive socially: fear of rejection, insecurity, self-esteem, lack of respect, and so on. You clearly want to feel comfortable and positive, but you can't seem to get there yet. In order to get into an emotional place where you can actively go out and feel comfortable and positive, you need to overcome emotional issues you may not even be aware you have. This is exactly how a therapist can help. They can help you overcome the problems you have, and the ones you don't even realize you have are the ones most likely stopping you from succeeding.

THE "WOW I NEVER REALIZED THAT" MOMENT

One summer when I was eighteen, I went on a weekend trip with a group of friends to a cabin we'd rented. I remember on two separate occasions on that weekend, I said two things I found to be stupid. I don't remember exactly what I said, since it was insignificant in and of itself, but I remember my friends' reactions. Some of them were probably wishing I hadn't said what I said. They might have forgotten about it after a few moments, but I didn't, at least at the time. Those two instances killed my mood for the entire trip and left me sort of anxious and on edge. I think the reason this happened is because I experienced such a negative reaction from the people around me, a "Why would you say that" type of thing.

I was in such a negative mental state of self-hatred after the weekend trip that I signed up for an online therapy service because I knew something was up. All I did was say something I should have laughed off or cringingly let go. Clearly, this type of mental state was not beneficial.

After being assigned a counselor, we did the usual things: talked about why I was there, talked about who I was, talked about how I felt, and so on. Then we got into the good stuff.

I explained to my counselor that I'd been experiencing problems with saying something I perceived to be stupid and receiving a negative response. When this happened, I'd immediately close down and start beating myself up. She agreed with me that I had a problem, so we started digging deeper. We talked about my university experience, the positive and the negative, although I definitely perceived it to be more negative. A few problems, but still not the core—we moved on. We started talking about my high-school life—more positives—but then, we dove into some negative experiences. I told her that I had a pretty good high-school life. It wasn't exactly eventful or anything, but I had a solid group of friends and we had fun.

But there was definitely a gaping hole for as long as I could remember—my love life. I'd never really been that successful with girls for . . . pretty much my entire life. My parents weren't exactly great teachers for how to succeed with teenage girls I liked, because they grew up in a different country with completely different social norms. My siblings, by extension, were in the same boat as me. My friends were probably struggling equally. I guess it was no surprise that I didn't have a great love life—or any love life, for that matter.

My counselor and I started investigating this. She was pretty sure this was the root of my problems. I wasn't convinced, but hey, I'm not the one with the credentials. She asked me if I ever tried to date any girls I liked in high school. Aha, well, dang . . . the answer is yes, unfortunately.

I was in ninth grade when I first experienced feelings for a girl. It was my first year of high school, and I was meeting people from elementary schools all over the town (the town didn't have middle schools). I had a few crushes on girls in my elementary school, but they were more childhood fantasies than anything. But in ninth grade, I met this one girl and developed feelings for her. Of course, I was fourteen at the time, so I had absolutely no clue what to do.

I talked to her quite a bit throughout the semester. I added her on Facebook, and we chatted in person quite a bit, too. I thought things were going great—I mean, she was replying to my messages and she seemed happy in person, so that must have meant I was on the right track, right? (Note my extreme naiveté.) It didn't help that a guy I also knew was super into her, too. Although I was sure I was a better option than him, my eagerness to date her became an urgent matter. I didn't want to run the risk of losing her to this guy.

After a few more weeks of talking, both in person and on Facebook, I messaged her and told her that I liked her. It was nothing too serious—I just dropped it casually into a conversation we were having. She continued the conversation without acknowledging what I had said. Maybe she didn't see it (Tak in ninth grade clearly couldn't take a hint).

I was confused, but I carried on naively. A few weeks after that, I told her again that I liked her, but this time I was more direct, so my message couldn't be overlooked. Well, I guess my intent worked, because she gave me a straight response this time. Unfortunately for me, the straight answer was not the one I wanted to know.

It went something along the lines of, "That's really sweet, but I don't feel the same way in return. I think we should just stay friends."

. . .

. . .

. . .

Oh.

. . .

Well . . . now what.

If the external world came crashing down at that moment, I wouldn't have noticed because my internal world had already crashed down with her response.

Of course, I felt extremely bad, but I played it cool, both to her and to myself. I didn't tell anyone what happened, I didn't get emotional about it, and I just carried on like nothing was wrong—despite the fact that I put my neck out and got my head chopped off and my emotional subconscious was probably running around in panic.

When I told my counselor this story, sure enough, we both realized this was the issue. How did I know this was the issue? I think the fact that I was pretty much in tears telling her this story had something to do with it. That was the first time I'd told anyone that story. Why had I never told anyone before? It took me six years to admit it, six years of pushing away and suppressing a devastating event and not properly dealing with it.

When my counselor explained why that event was affecting me all those years later, my mind was blown! I told a girl I liked her, she responded negatively, and I shut down and felt awful about myself. The same thing happened with those moments on the cabin trip. I said something stupid, people responded negatively, and I shut down and felt awful about myself. My reaction—shutting down and beating myself up—was just a psychological defense mechanism to prevent me from feeling the type of negative emotion I felt when I got rejected for the first time. I was subconsciously trying to protect myself from emotional pain, although I may have been doing a bad job.

This mental pattern had been building for the last six years because I never properly worked through those emotions. Well, I thought, better late than never. We were going to work through those emotions right now.

A big part of working through your emotions is talking about them. Just the act of talking about your emotions can solve many emotional problems. Storing away and suppressing your emotions is likely causing them to come up again, just in a different context. In my case, to put the nail in the coffin and put my emotional problem to rest, my therapist had me write out a letter to my ninth grade self. We discussed the letter in our following session.

> Letter to Younger Self: Exercise for Therapy. *Not edited, other than for minor grammatical changes. Some names removed for privacy.*
>
> Written: August 2018
> Events Occurred: School Year of 2012-13
> Hey ninth grade Tak, this is an older you coming to talk to you about what happened with (her name). First, I just want to reassure you that everything is going to be okay. Take it from me; I'm the living proof. I understand it wasn't easy to make yourself vulnerable and tell her how you felt about her, and I definitely understand how you felt when you got rejected, the feeling of embarrassment that you got from her and from other people if they found out although I don't think anyone did, the feeling of shame because you spent hours fantasizing about a relationship that seemed almost certain to be ripped out from under you, and the feeling of jealousy you felt when you found out another guy started dating

her. I don't blame you for having strong emotions either, because she was beautiful, had an amazing body, and was sweet.

I remember when you were in elementary school and you had huge crushes on three girls and never had the courage to let them know how you felt. When you did muster up the courage to let a girl know how you felt and got rejected, I know the pain you experienced. It didn't help that you didn't tell another girl you had a huge crush on that same year how you felt about her. And it really didn't help that the next year, you told another girl you had a huge crush on how you felt and experienced the same thing again. Also, the prom date rejection four years later in senior year probably made you feel like your whole high-school experience was not romantically successful. But I appreciate that you had the courage to ask out another girl you had an enormous crush on in the first year of university, despite all of the things you were going through, but when she didn't want a relationship, it made you feel like you were in ninth grade all over again.

I'm writing to you to thank you for protecting me all these years from more failure and rejection, but now that I am older, more mature and wiser, I will be able to handle rejections in order to go after what I really want in my dating life. I'm sorry that all those high-school experiences made you feel worthless in terms of your dating life and made

> you feel insecure about still being a virgin. But everything will be better; I can't tell you how because even I'm not sure, but I promise that everything will turn out better than you expected.

I'm proud to say that after writing this letter and talking about it in my next section, my mind was relieved, and all of a sudden, I stopped beating myself up for the stupid things I say. I still say stupid things; don't get me wrong, but I don't beat myself up for it nearly as much I did before dealing with my issues.

I tell you this story because therapy helped me work through this problem—including other issues like this—that I most likely would've never worked through on my own. As a young, inexperienced person looking at myself through my first-person view, I never would've been able to figure out the root of my problems and make the connection.

Therapy is a great place for you to express your emotions in a safe, private space with a trained professional, but sometimes the benefit comes from someone asking you the right questions for the first time. Trust me, if you're dealing with any social issues—and you most likely are, given the fact that you're reading this book—I would highly recommend talking to a therapist. You may also find yourself working through issues from roots you never thought you had.

Your problems most likely differ from mine, but all problems share the same fundamental outline: we have suppressed emotions we haven't worked through, which causes problems in our present day. Whether those problems affect your perception of yourself after a negative reaction from someone else like they did me—whether it's a self-perception issue, a distorted view of something, or an inability to be social, assertive, or comfortable—therapy is a great tool for moving past what's keeping you stuck.

However, therapy is only a tool. You get out what you put into it, kind of like at the gym. You don't just buy a gym membership and show up and expect to be slim and muscular; you have to put in the consistent work through effort. It's the same with therapy, except the effort is about showing up and expressing your emotions, which means being vulnerable. This can be really hard for some people because vulnerability requires you to fight through emotional pain, but that's the whole point. It's a safe, private space with a trained person for a reason—so you can work through your issues safely and privately.

Key Takeaways

- The principle in this chapter of improving your social life is making other people feel comfortable and positive. The reason you need to make people feel comfortable and positive is because those are the two basic feelings one must have in order to feel safe, and this is the most basic feeling one needs in order to enjoy their interactions with you.
- The key in making someone feel comfortable and positive around you is to make yourself feel comfortable and positive.
- To learn to be comfortable, you must address social anxiety. You can do this by overcoming the fear of rejection, identifying and challenging beliefs, addressing insecurities, and focusing on the interaction.
- To learn to feel positive, you must learn to respect yourself. You can do this by being personally congruent, setting and enforcing strong boundaries, and feeling your feelings freely.
- Working with a therapist can help you work through any issues you have in this chapter, or with life in general.

CHAPTER 8

Social Skills

The second presidential debate of 1992 between US President George. H. W. Bush and Governor Bill Clinton of Arkansas was one of the most memorable moments of the general election. It would highlight to the world the social expertise of the new president. Bill Clinton is the epitome of charisma and social skill. Even regular people have said that when you talked to President Clinton, it felt like the whole world stopped and it was just you and him because he would stop, give you his complete and undivided attention, and talk to you in a way that made you feel like his good friend.

During the Q&A portion of the event, a lady was given the microphone and asked Bush her question. Bush got up from his seat, which was about thirty feet away from her, and started to answer. He was clearly caught off guard by her question because he bumbled around for a bit and started answering a question that wasn't exactly what she asked. When another person stepped in and clarified her original question,

Bush did what he could to answer. Addressing the crowd as a whole, he gave a fairly solid answer, although it wasn't necessarily memorable. Clinton had the chance to answer the same question. He got out of the seat that was beside Bush and immediately walked right up to the woman to answer her question. He related to her question, shared a few touching stories about his experiences, and answered her question with exceptional delivery and professionalism. The whole time he was talking, he didn't break eye contact to look at another person, even though there was a decent-sized crowd to whom he could've turned his attention. The woman was fully engaged in her interaction with Clinton and appeared extremely satisfied with the answer.

Regardless of his politics or his scandals, there is no denying that Bill Clinton is a master of social skills. You don't need to be the leader of the free world to have this level of social skill—it can be developed with practice and habit.

Strong social skills are paramount to your success in being social because how you speak represents how well you can communicate everything going on internally. However, I put this chapter near the end of the self-improvement part of this book, as a lot of people's social problems are caused not because they lack true social skills, but because of all the other internal issues they face. Your problem may not be that you don't know what to say; it may be the fear of rejection. Your problem may not be that you aren't funny, but that you may lack mental sharpness as a result of poor health.

However, becoming socially competent is important, and this chapter is dedicated to helping you improve.

Small Talk Is Not Boring If You're Not

To some people, small talk can seem boring, shallow, and unnecessary, but it's far more important than you may consciously realize.

Let's say a random man you've never met before is introduced to you at a party. After shaking hands and exchanging names, he immediately starts telling you how his dog died last weekend and he had to cancel his plans with his friends because he was too occupied grieving and crying over the loss of his dog. How would you react? While you may feel sorry for him, you probably won't be able to help thinking, "What is wrong with this guy?"

This is exactly why small talk is so important. Small talk allows people to establish a sense of commonality and to share and gather information about each other. The information you gather allows you to assess whether the person to whom you're speaking is a threat or not. It also allows you to assess their social status, their emotional stability, their mood, and everything that is important to feeling safe and to building a connection.

Let's say that same dogless man was introduced to you at a party and he started the conversation with small talk. The interaction could have opened a window for both of you to be vulnerable, if you were comfortable enough with each other to do so.

Small talk is important, but it can be boring if one or both of you suck at it. Here's how to brighten up your boring small talk.

HOW TO BE SOCIALLY ENTERTAINING

Small talk usually won't consist of super deep emotions. Mostly, it will be lighthearted, shallow, and fun. Nevertheless, it's still extremely important. Learning how to be socially engaging will make whomever you're speaking with more receptive to you and will further friendship.

The "Yes and. . ." Mentality

The "yes and. . . " mentality means you take a conversational thread and add something on to it.

Think of it like playing tennis. For a tennis game to be fun, both players need to keep hitting the ball back and forth. One person serves (starts a conversational topic), and the other hits the ball back (good reply), and they go back and forth building on each person's reply. If you take a look at any good, free-flowing conversation, both people are following this exact principle, whether they know it or not.

Example of a "yes and . . ." conversation about sports:

- A: Do you watch any sports?
- B: Yeah, I watch basketball.
- A: Man, did you see Kawhi's game winner against the Sixers?
- B: That was awesome! They're going all the way this year.
- Conversation continues. . .

Notice how each person added to what the other person said? This would naturally continue until someone brings up another topic of conversation, and they go again from there.

Of course, in this example, the person had knowledge of the topic of conversation—basketball—but the same principle holds true, even if one isn't too knowledgeable about the topic.

Example of a "yes and . . ." conversation about sports, but one person isn't as knowledgeable:

- A: Do you watch any sports?
- B: I watch sports here and there but don't really follow.
- A: You should've seen it yesterday. Kawhi Leonard from the Toronto Raptors hit a game winner against the Sixers in the last game of the playoff series. The ball was bouncing around the rim and finally went in, and the crowd went crazy.
- B: I wish I saw that. What happens now?
- A: Now the Raptors play the Milwaukee Bucks.
- B: Who do you think wins that?
- Conversation continues . . .

The opposite of a "yes and . . ." conversation is when someone gives an answer that doesn't add on to anything the other person mentioned, and the burden of restarting the conversation goes back to the person who started the topic initially.

A fun, free-flowing conversation is like a tennis game where both people are hitting the ball back and forth after one person serves, but a conversation where someone gives a boring, flat answer is like serving the ball . . . and no one's there, so you have to run over to the other side of the court, pick up your ball, run back to your side, and serve again. That is a very lonely game that the person will leave sooner rather than later.

Example of a conversation that the other person doesn't add to:

- A: Do you watch any sports?
- B: Not really.

- A: What do you usually watch?
- B: I don't usually watch anything.

You might laugh when you read this example. But this type of conversation is extremely common. If it wasn't such a big problem, I wouldn't be writing this.

Be Knowledgeable

Conversations using the second example of the "yes and . . ." mentality are good for when you don't know what the topic of conversation is about. But if most of the conversation with the other person is like that, it will also become a boring conversation, since it will seem like a one-sided explanation of various topics. Most people like explaining and teaching things to people, but not for the majority of the conversation or friendship.

Going back to our tennis analogy, a conversation where one person is knowledgeable and the other is not is like Roger Federer playing against an infant. Roger is going to blast 117-mph serves and the infant isn't going to hit any balls back, so there is virtually no chance of a fun back and forth.

Being knowledgeable doesn't require you to be a walking-talking Google or have five doctorate degrees, but it means you know enough about what you're talking about. Ideally, you should have several topics you know inside out and also about a wide range of topics.

The range of being knowledgeable includes:

- Being an expert on the topic: you know a lot about the subject and you can explain virtually anything about it to anyone.

- Being educated on the topic: you know enough about the conversation to offer interesting perspectives and to share information.
- Being conversational about the topic: you know enough about the topic to hold your own in a conversation.
- Being ignorant about the topic: you don't know much about the topic.

Common topics of conversation include:

- Sports
    - Hockey
    - Basketball
    - American football
    - Baseball
    - Football (soccer)
    - Boxing / mixed martial arts
- Politics
- World events
- Movies and television shows
- Video games
- Books
- Podcasts
- Business
- Career
- Finance
- Health and fitness
- Music
- The city/town you live in
- Food

- Alcohol
- Celebrities
- Travel
- Children
- Restaurants
- Cars
- Coffee/tea
- Cooking
- Clothes
- Shopping
- Goals and habits
- Social media
- Self-improvement
- Languages
- Animals
- History
- Psychology
- Law
- Science
- Religion
- Dating/sex

Humor

People connect very strongly over shared laughter. Think about all the best moments you've had with your friends—many of those moments involved you two laughing and enjoying yourselves, right?

Humor is a way for us to laugh, enjoy ourselves, and connect, but it's not that complicated. You don't need to be a Dave

Chappelle or a Kevin Hart who makes stadiums full of people laugh with every other sentence—a few funny moments throughout an interaction is all you need.

Rules of Humor

Humor, like anything else, does not happen by accident. There are certain rules that make humor effective.

COMMIT TO THE HUMOR

Something that makes people extremely funny is their commitment to humor.

If you watch any good stand-up comedian, you'll notice that when they're telling a story or a joke, they are fully committed to the delivery. Everything from their vocal tonality, facial expression, and body language is part of the joke.

What do people who aren't funny do? They say their joke half-heartedly (or don't even say it at all), which results in them not being funny. The difference between them and the Dave Chappelles of the world (aside from talent) is vulnerability.

Comedians are extremely socially vulnerable when they're on stage. They are fully committed to telling a joke, and if it falls flat and the audience doesn't laugh, they can look like a complete fool on stage. They are willing to do this because they know that the full commitment to their joke is what makes the joke funny in the first place. People who aren't funny hedge their bets by being duller and less enthusiastic, which works even further against them.

Being committed to your humor doesn't necessarily mean you're crazy, loud, and over-the-top, it just means you are telling jokes without hesitation, also known as being socially vulnerable. Kevin Hart is super crazy and over-the-top when he is committing to a joke or a skit, but Dave Chappelle is often pretty calm and relaxed. Both are extremely funny people.

DON'T OVERDO HUMOR

Overdoing humor can be just as annoying as not being humorous at all. Unless you can be funny without putting much effort into it, or you have a funny personality, don't seek to overdo the humor.

Being constantly funny works great if the majority of the things you say are funny, which comes with experience, talent, and a certain personality, but if you're working on becoming funny, just worry about being funny a few times as opposed to trying to do a one-hour Netflix comedy special.

MAKE YOURSELF LAUGH

Otherwise referred to as self-amusement, this is when you focus on making yourself laugh, which invites the other person to laugh too. This reduces your need to be socially vulnerable because you're not depending on the other person to make your joke succeed. You simply tell a story or joke, which makes you laugh and enjoy yourself, and then the other person can join in on your laughter if they find it funny too.

MAKE THEM FEEL INCLUDED

People love humor when they feel like they're in on the joke, not when they're the butt of the joke. You can be funny and be a complete asshole, or you can be funny and supercharge your connection. The difference is who is at the butt of the joke. If either no one or you, yourself, are the joke, then it's funny and inclusive, since you and the person or people you're trying to make laugh are laughing together. But if the person or people you're trying to make laugh are the victims of the joke, the situation becomes threatening and standoffish.

Jokes and stories that don't have to do with the other person should be fine for the most part, but if you are going to joke about the other person, keep the humor either neutral or build them up; don't push them down. If someone has messy hair today, you can joke that the hair makes them look more badass if they put on a really nice suit and pretend to be the boss anytime they walk into the room (builds them up). Or you can say something like: they're looking closer and closer to the Joker with every passing day (neutral, depending on how it's delivered). But if you say something like: it looks like someone shaved your hair and put a dead raccoon on your head, this is obviously quite insulting.

This is why self-deprecation is so effective. Self-deprecation makes the joke teller the victim of the joke and allows the other people to laugh with you, while you laugh at yourself. If the joke teller had messy hair, then saying something like "It looks like someone shaved my hair and put a dead raccoon on my head" could be pretty funny.

Self-deprecating humor works well if the joke teller is someone who is confident and/or of a high status, since the joke brings them down a notch and makes them feel more relatable, but if the person is already quite depressive, unconfident, or makes too many self-deprecating jokes, it can just be sad. Self-deprecating humor follows the other rule of humor: don't overdo it.

If you do end up making a joke that seeks to put someone down, also known as a diss, roast, or tease, make sure to go about it in a socially intelligent way. This means, be careful of what you joke about. Make sure you're not laughing at the expense of someone else's insecurities. Nothing will kill a potential friendship faster than laughing at someone else's insecurities, whether the person making the joke was intentionally hurtful or not.

How to Be Funny

There could be an entire book or course created on how to be funny, but we'll outline three common humor tactics used by everyone from your funny uncle, famous comedians, to people like you and me.

SAYING THE UNEXPECTED

When someone tells us a story or a joke, our brains naturally try and anticipate what they'll say next, but saying the unexpected breaks that pattern, which shocks our brains and makes us laugh as a result.

To illustrate the point about anticipation, pretend you're in this conversation:

- You: Hey Mark, how's it going?
- Mark: I'm doing well. What's up with you?
- You: Just reading this great book on leading a social life. Did you catch that basketball game last night?
- Mark: Yeah! That game-winning dunk was crazy.

- You: I can't believe how tall people in the NBA are.
- Mark: Yeah, I heard some people breed with giraffes in an attempt to make their kids taller.

Wasn't that funny? When you said, "I can't believe how tall people in the NBA are," you were expecting Mark to respond with something along the lines of tall people in the NBA, but nope . . . he was talking about human baby giraffes. Obviously, Mark isn't being serious, but his saying the unexpected would've made anyone laugh.

EXAGGERATION

Exaggeration is when you take something either normal or slightly funny and blow it out of proportion. The joke is in the exaggeration of the original topic. This is funny because it is unexpected, but also because exaggeration makes things sound ridiculous.

Examples of exaggeration could be:

- "My coffee doesn't taste very good today."
    - "Yeah, I don't think the slaves who harvested the beans cared if it tasted good or not." (Dark humor, but still funny.)
- "The Seahawks are going to the Super Bowl this year!"
    - "Yeah, I think they'll win more than one game!" (Understatements are a form of exaggeration.)
- "I died laughing at that movie."
    - "Same! My mom was about to call the coffin store telling them they were about to get a new customer."

PLAYING A CHARACTER

This one is my favorite. Playing a character is either when you imitate somebody or something to make an example, when you exaggerate something another person said, or when you say the unexpected.

The key to playing a character is to make your vocal tonality different, so the other person knows that you're switching roles. If you're going to play a character well, make sure you commit fully to playing the character. If you're going to imitate a movie character, for example, commit fully. You don't want a half character, half real person. This ruins the whole point of being a character.

It would be extremely difficult to write out how to play a different character, but watch pretty much any comedian, since they play different characters many times during their shows. Notice their commitment to the character.

Not Just Questions

If you keep bombarding the other person with questions, it may start feeling like a corporate job interview more than a fun conversation.

Mix it up by making statements instead of constantly questioning. Statements give the other person an opportunity to add into the conversation at their own will, which could lead to them investing more in the conversation and/or bringing up some new perspectives.

Examples of turning questions into statements include:

- Instead of asking someone what they're going to do this weekend, share what you will do.

- Instead of asking someone what they do for work, share something cool that you do.
- Instead of asking someone a question to get over an awkward silence, make a comment on something.

Storytelling

One alternative to talking in questions and statements is to tell a story. Humans are designed to be fascinated by stories, connect over sharing stories, and learn very well through stories.

These are some of the reasons why I include multiple stories in my chapters: to keep you reading, to better connect with you, and to help you learn. You may or may not remember facts, but you will certainly understand them if I tell an interesting story to go along with them. This is also the reason why you probably love to read stories, watch movies and TV shows, and play video games: because they all are variations of stories. Everything from *Thomas the Tank Engine* to *Assassin's Creed* video games are stories.

Pretty much all stories share the same general pattern. Stories can be of varying lengths and what you include in each part is up to you, but they're all similarly structured:

- Introduction: Introduce the context and the people involved.
- Buildup: Build up the details and tell the story leading up to the main point.
- Climax: This is the main point of the story—the big, dramatic moment of the story or the main idea you want to get across.
    - Alternatively, consider the anticlimax. An anticlimax is when the listener has been built up to expect

a big climax, but instead the climax turns out to be something insignificant and/or unexpected, which can also make for a great story.

- Winding down: This doesn't happen for all stories, but after the climax, you can start to close the gaps and prepare the listeners for the conclusion.
    - Alternatively, repeat the buildup. Some stories don't just have one main point. If there are multiple, repeat the buildup after the first climax.
- Conclusion: This is where you signal to the listener that the story is over.

A Five-Thousand-to-One Odds That Actually Happens

In this section, we will break down a story into the different parts we've just discussed.

(Introduction) Leicester City F.C. is an English professional football (soccer) club, but to be frank, they were never historically relevant to the world football stage. In the 2013–14 season, they won the English Football League Championship, England's second highest overall football league, which meant that next season they would be promoted to the top league, the English Premier League.

The next season wouldn't be much different. The 2014–15 season would conclude with Leicester City F.C. coming in fourteenth place out of twenty clubs—below average, but nothing out of the ordinary for a club who had never experienced much success previously.

(Buildup) The betting odds for the 2015–16 Premier League season reflected Leicester City's chances of success.

Bookmakers had Leicester City F.C. at five-thousand-to-one odds for winning the Premier League that season. To put this in perspective, England's top bookmaker, William Hill, offered five-thousand-to-one odds that President Barack Obama would play cricket for England once he vacated the White House. Yes, an American President playing cricket for England and a football club winning a football championship had the same probability of happening.

(Climax) And then it started to happen. They started to win . . . a lot. They consistently beat their fellow Premier League clubs, drew many crucial matches with top ranked clubs (draws still count for a point), and lost only three matches out of thirty-eight to win the Premier League for the first time in history. This is often described as one of the greatest sporting stories of all time.

(Winding down) I feel kind of bad for the bookmakers. They are likely not going to ever give out five-thousand-to-one odds for football anymore. One Leicester City F.C. fan who bet £50 ended up cashing out his bet early for £72,000. He stood to win £250,000 if he saw his bet through to the end of the season.

(Conclusion) Wouldn't it be crazy if that ever happened again?

Deeper Conversations Build Connection

Although we discussed why small talk is important for your social skills, you can't rely on just small talk. You will eventually need to get into deeper conversation if you want to build real connections.

WHEN TO HAVE DEEPER CONVERSATION

There is no hard and fast rule on when small talk ends and when you are allowed to transition into deep conversation. The best rule of thumb is when you're comfortable enough with the other person. Although this is mostly a subconscious feeling, if you were to measure comfort with another person, it would be by how much you trust them.

Trust may take a long time to build with some people you meet, but for others, trust can be developed within the first interaction. There are people I've known for years that I don't trust, so I still stick with small talk when I speak to them, but there are people I've just met who seemed open, friendly, and trustworthy enough that I was comfortable enough to at least start testing the waters of deep conversation.

HOW TO TRANSITION TO DEEPER CONVERSATION

Transitioning to deeper conversations isn't a specific phase or procedure. It's when you introduce topics of conversations that are more personal and that allow you to get to know the other person better, and vice versa.

You can do this by changing the topic of conversation, telling a deeper story, asking for someone's opinion on something personal, raising deeper questions, or providing some knowledgeable insight. You start sharing slightly deeper things, and if you and the person with whom you're speaking click on that level, you can go a level deeper, then continue progressing as long as both of you are comfortable with it.

Let's say there are a hundred levels to a conversation, level one being shallow conversation and level one hundred being your deepest secret you haven't told anyone. When you're transitioning from small talk to deeper conversation, it doesn't make sense for you to share level fifty- or sixty-type type information yet. You start out by sharing things that are around levels one to five, such as something that happened at work or a small problem you're dealing with at home. These moments of slight vulnerability let the person know that you have layers to you that go past the surface-level interaction you're having. It's a good start to opening the door for deeper conversation at a later time.

Deep conversation is also a two-way street. If you have hung out with someone multiple times and you're sharing level-twenty-type things at this point and the other person is still at a level three, there is a disconnect that will inevitably lead to an awkward relationship. If you're sharing things in a reasonable, socially calibrated manner, it may very well be that the other person is not capable of being emotionally vulnerable, which is far more common than you may realize.

Aside from sharing deeper details such as life dreams or sensitive secrets, deeper conversation also comes when you start understanding why people do things and how they feel. Understanding why allows you to learn more about other people's values, thoughts, and opinions; learning about their feelings allows you to connect with them, since connection is about being emotionally connected, not logically connected.

Miscellaneous Social Skills

There are a number of important miscellaneous social skills that you will have to learn in order to be able to have great conversations, whether it be during small talk or deeper conversation.

AWKWARD SILENCES

If you're going to have conversations with people, silences are inevitable. The question is, is the silence going to be awkward? If you get into a silence and you rush to fill it or stare awkwardly at the other person and at your surroundings, then the other person will mirror your internal state. This is what awkward silences are—when the people are awkward in the silence, not the silence itself.

Just understanding that silences will happen is a giant step. This may sound obvious when you read it. But think about it in your own life. When silence happens, do you feel like you're obligated to fill it? You don't need to be super connected with the other person to a point where every second is filled with noise. If awkward thoughts come up, be mindful of them, acknowledge, investigate, and accept them, then go back to talking when you feel ready. The other person is probably having the same kinds of thoughts.

KEEPING A CONVERSATION GOING

Earlier in the book, we discussed that asking how to keep a conversation going is the wrong way to frame your problem, which is true. Most conversations that don't flow well have to do with either person or both not being comfortable enough with each other to continue introducing new topics. Assuming that you are comfortable enough with the other person, there are still tactical errors that lead to conversations stalling out.

We discussed in the small-talk section the importance of not giving boring, flat answers, but instead using the "yes and . . ." mentality to continue adding things to say. There are a number of other tactics you can use to continue the conversation.

BE INTERESTED . . . AND BE INTERESTING

Common conversation advice given by friends, family, the internet, or the classic self-help book, *How to Win Friends and Influence People* by Dale Carnegie, says to ask people about themselves and get them talking about themselves. This can work, but for a real conversation with real connection to happen, both people need to be sharing the conversational burden.

Conversation Branching

Almost every naturally flowing conversation works according to the following: one person says something, the other person responds to that subject, they go back and forth, one person starts another conversational topic related to the one they first talked about, and repeat.

For example, if someone says:

- "Last summer, my friends and I went on a camping trip where we got really drunk and told funny stories around a campfire."

You can talk about any of the related topics the other person said. I call this conversation branching. You can most certainly ask the other person about their camping trip, but if you want to talk, you can branch off and talk about your own experiences.

With that same line, you can talk about the following:

- "Last summer, my friends and I went on a camping trip where we got really drunk and told funny stories around a campfire."
    - "I spent the entirety of last summer working."
    - "My friends and I once took a weekend trip to Montreal."
    - "The last time I went on a camping trip . . ."
    - "Once I got really drunk and . . ."
    - "I have a funny story . . ."
    - "I have a great campfire story . . ."

Topic Changers

You don't have to have an exact, logical chain of topics in mind in order to talk about things. If you're comfortable enough with the other person, you can most certainly jump off into another topic, story, or question by using topic changers such as "reminds me of," "one time," "kind of random, but," etc.

- "That reminds me of one time my friends, and I went to get Italian food and they were out of pizza. What kind of Italian place is out of pizza?"
- "One time I went grocery shopping and forgot my wallet. I had to have the grocery store keep my items on hold, while I took a bus home, got my wallet, bussed there, then took an Uber home."

- "This is kind of random, but what country would you travel to if you could pick?"

ENDING CONVERSATIONS

Every conversation you enter will have to be left eventually. For conversations that don't come to a natural end at a convenient time, you will have to choose to leave when you want to. The best conversation endings are ones that feel socially calibrated and don't make the other person feel like you're leaving them abruptly.

You must understand that it's okay to end a conversation and leaving doesn't mean you hate the other person.

You can end a conversation by signaling or by verbally leaving. Signaling is when you indirectly communicate that you're done with the conversation. Common signals include starting to turn your body away from the other person; answering in shorter, less engaging words; checking your phone; or not contributing to the conversation. You can also resume what you were doing before. If you were working on something, you can calmly go back to working on it.

If the other person doesn't end the conversation after you signal, or you don't want to signal and want to verbally tell them you're ending the conversation, you can use the following phrases:

- "It was good seeing you; I'm going to head out now."
- "Anyway, I should get going."
- "If you'll excuse me, I have to get to _____."
- "It was good seeing you, I should get back to _____."

GROUP CONVERSATIONS

Group conversations have different dynamics compared to one-on-one conversations, since group conversations are a collection of all of the participants' social behavior. In group interactions, you don't need to light up the entire conversation. There is less pressure, since other people can carry the conversational burden. But the challenge is usually how not to stay quiet.

You can contribute to the conversation by adding in interesting conversational topics like any social interaction, or you can simply add responses, since you don't carry 50 percent of the conversational burden.

Group conversations are harder to get a chance to speak, since there are multiple people trying to contribute to the conversation instead of you and another person. The best times to add your contribution is when there is silence or after someone says something. When you do speak up, make sure to commit completely to your words and say them with conviction. Words that are backed up with a strong, respectable presence don't usually get interrupted, and when they do, they still get acknowledged. It's when you enter the conversation quietly and weakly that you get interrupted or talked over.

NONVERBAL COMMUNICATION

Nonverbal communication is a significant part of social interactions. It's one of the reasons why digital forms of communication such as social media, text, and email don't compare to being face-to-face with someone.

Entire chapters or books could be written about nonverbal communication. There are a few simple things you can do to help improve your nonverbal communication, but here's the general principle: nonverbal communication is a reflection of your internal state. Sure, you can tell someone to smile more and make eye contact with them, but that usually comes naturally to most people when they feel comfortable and positive.

In this chapter, we are looking to tighten tactical gaps in your social skills. If you find yourself struggling greatly with improving aspects of nonverbal communication, chances are it's an internal problem, since nonverbal communication is strongly influenced by your inner state. If this is the case for you, go back to Chapter 7 and work on feeling comfortable and positive.

Smile and Laugh Openly

A lot of people who struggle socially also struggle with expressing themselves properly. Learning to smile and laugh openly and with a sense of freedom opens you up to feeling more comfortable and positive, makes the other person more interested in you (since you are signaling interest in the interaction and in them), and causes the other person to do the same due to mirroring.

When building this into a habit, work on smiling openly first before moving into laughing, since smiling openly naturally leads to laughing openly, but laughing openly without smiling can come off as socially uncalibrated.

This isn't about fake laughing or being ingenuine, but about opening yourself up to a point where you can laugh easier when the opportunities allow for it.

Eye Contact

Eye contact is key to building trust and intimacy with others, but there is a balance. As a general rule, keep good eye contact, but don't stare.

Body Language

Your body language is a reflection of your internal state and signals how you're feeling towards other people. If you're presenting negative body language to another person but your internal state is positive, the other person will get mixed signals but may easily end up interpreting the negative over the positive, as we usually, instinctively do.

Facing the other person, carrying strong posture, and opening up your body language are among the most impactful things you can do when it comes to communicating through your body. You don't need to follow these body language or nonverbal rules 100 percent of the time, but you should use them as often as possible.

Face the other person when possible, or, put better, avoid facing away from them. There are instances where you obviously can't face someone, such as when you're walking or sitting in certain places, and that's fine—it's sometimes even beneficial, since facing directly in front of someone can be seen as confrontational. But you want to avoid facing away from the other person. This will help to communicate that you're receptive and interested.

Carrying strong posture helps other people respect you and perceive you as more confident, since you are carrying your body in a way that conveys external and internal strength.

Stand up with your back straight, shoulders back, and head straight.

Last but not least, shift your body language. Open body language means free-flowing arms, revealing your torso area, and exposing your neck. Closed body language means crossing your arms, making yourself as small as possible, and keeping your head tucked. Open body language signals that you're not perceiving the other person as a threat.

Social Intelligence

Social intelligence is the type of intelligence that can either support or prevent well-intentioned people from developing connections with other people. Without social intelligence, even good, kind, well-meaning people may not be able to create fulfilling social relationships.

Being social can be summarized by understanding people and behaving accordingly. The general principle in regard to creating a social life is to understand what other people think and how they feel, and to be aware of how you affect their thoughts and feelings.

DON'T CRITICIZE OTHER PEOPLE

The most obvious principle to follow when it comes to understanding what other people think and feel is not to directly create negative feelings in them. Negative feelings often come in the form of criticism. Criticism affects the other person's self-image because their identity and what they believe to be true about themselves (being smart, good, right, etc.) is directly challenged.

Unless you absolutely need to point out something critical about someone, refrain from doing so. If you find yourself being overly critical of others, it most likely has to do with judgments of yourself that you haven't worked through yet. Instead of dealing with them internally, you try to project them outwards.

BE AWARE OF PEOPLE'S INSECURITIES

One of the biggest sources of people's negative thoughts are their insecurities. Criticizing someone can easily reveal their insecurities, so this is another reason not to criticize, but it goes further than that. You can easily trigger a person's insecurities unintentionally or without even doing anything. Some of the best, kindest people in the world can trigger people's insecurities quite easily, whether it's by something they said that wasn't even directed at them, or the fact that they represent something that the other person wants but doesn't have. Control what you can control in these cases. You can control what you say and what you do, but if you represent something that sparks someone else's insecurities, it isn't your fault; it's just a mismatch.

A list of possible things people can be insecure about include:

- Health
- Physical appearance
- Job
- Money
- Social status
- Intelligence
- Social ability
- Mental state
- Romantic relationship

- Friendships
- Sexual history
- Age
- Lack of independence
- Upbringing
- Embarrassing things they've done

VALIDATE OTHERS

Humans have a craving to be validated by others. Validation is a huge part of the primal social connection we create because validation directly signals to the other person that we like them and accept them. Validation is the complete opposite of feeling lonely, since loneliness is the lack of connection.

When people are in any sort of interaction with each other, assuming they get past the phase where they don't see each other as a threat, the thing going through their minds is, "Do they like me?" This is why we put on our best selves for people we've just met, why we post pictures on social media, and why we do nice things for others—because we need to know if people like us or not.

People with high internal security can go a bit longer without direct validation, but nevertheless, humans are still human—we all need validation. This isn't just limited to the first time you give someone validation, although that is a big step in any relationship. People need constant reassurance that they are liked by other people. Try not giving your partner any more validation, since you've already given them enough in the past and see how long that works out; it probably wouldn't last.

Validating others can include:

- Listening actively and making them feel heard
- Engaging with their thoughts or opinions
- Giving them compliments
- Doing thoughtful acts
- Calling them your friend
- Directly telling them you like them

ACTIVE LISTENING

I firmly believe that the most important part of conversation is what you do to listen. Everybody loves to talk, and many people are good at talking, but your ability to listen well is what will make the interactions far better and make people feel important.

Active listening is the key to making your interactions more fulfilling. Active listening is focusing intently on the other person and showing them you are present.

First, start with moving distractions. When you are listening to someone, you're focusing on them and nothing else. You're not looking over in the distance, looking at other people, or checking or scrolling through your phone. Of course, this, like anything else in this section, doesn't mean you follow this rule every single second, but take it as a general principle.

Next is to show you're present and direct your attention toward them. Removing distractions clears one hurdle, but the next step is to intently focus on the other person. This means you should turn your body towards them (if possible), maintain strong eye contact, listen to what they're saying, and stay present in the conversation.

MAKE SOMEONE FEEL HEARD

This one is the natural next step to active listening. Without active listening, it's impossible to make someone feel heard. When someone feels heard, it essentially means they feel understood.

When someone feels understood, they feel like the other person understands what they're saying but also *why* they're saying it. This concept is what marriage researcher Dr. John Gottman calls bids for emotion. A bid for emotion is when a partner does or says something in hopes of getting a positive emotional response from their partner.

When one partner puts out an emotional bid, the other partner has three options: turn toward the emotional bid and response positively, turn away from the emotional bid and respond negatively, or ignore it (or not even notice it).

Dr. Gottman's research is no joke. He has spent forty years studying marriages and is able to predict whether or not a couple will get divorced with 83-percent accuracy. Dr. Gottman has found that those who are masters at their relationship respond positively 86 percent of the time, while those who are disasters at their relationship respond positively only 33 percent of the time. He notes that the main reason couples break up or get divorced isn't a single, big event like a major fight or infidelity, but instead it's the growing resentment one or both partners build up when emotional bids get consistently ignored or turned away.

As bad as it is to turn away from a bid, the worst is when you ignore or even miss the bid. At least when someone turns away, the other person feels heard and maybe even understood—it just comes with a negative reaction. But when emotional bids are ignored, the person doesn't feel heard or understood at all.

Did they ignore me on purpose? Did they even hear what I said? Is my partner tuning me out? All of these questions can float in the head of the partner who got their bid ignored.

Although Dr. Gottman primarily focuses on marital relationships, his work is not by any means exclusive to people with rings on their fingers. The same concept applies to your dating relationships, family, friendships, relationships with coworkers or peers, and people you just met, because all relationships are human relationships.

Emotional bids can be either direct or indirect. Direct bids are when someone makes a direct, obvious attempt to get your positive attention, while indirect bids are when someone is subtle or passive. Caring about the other person and being present are two prerequisites for catching emotional bids. You want to aim to catch eight out of ten emotional bids. This can be a steep challenge, but that's the effort one must put into building strong relationships. The good news is that if you care about the other person and are present, you're probably catching a good amount of them.

Examples of Emotional Bids:

Direct bids

- "Hey, do you want to get something to eat?"
    - Turning toward:
        - "Sure! Let's go get pizza."
        - "Not right now, but thanks for offering!"
    - Turning away:
        - "Ok. Whatever."
        - "I'm good."

- "How was your day?"
    - Turning toward:
        - "My day was good!" *Explains day.*
        - "I didn't have a great day." *Explains day.*
    - Turning away:
        - "Good."
        - "Not bad."
- "Can we talk about (insert problem)?"
    - Turning toward:
        - "Sure, what's on your mind?"
    - Turning away:
        - "Why do we have to talk about that?"
        - "Come on, it's not that serious."
- "Check out this cool video!"
    - Turning toward:
        - *Comes over to see.*
    - Turning away:
        - "I'm busy."
        - "I'm good."

Indirect bids

- "I'm really bored."
    - Turning toward:
        - "Yeah, me too. Want to go do something?"
    - Turning away:
        - "Same."
        - "Yeah?"
- "LeBron James is such a good basketball player."
    - Turning toward:

    - "Yeah, he's awesome."
    - "Definitely! Do you think the Lakers are winning the NBA championship this year?"
- Turning away:
    - "I think he sucks, and I don't understand why you watch basketball so much; it's stupid."

SHARE THE MORE IMPORTANT DETAILS

As the classic saying goes, "A person's favorite topic of conversation is themselves." People like talking about themselves because it accomplishes many social goals. Talking about themselves makes them feel important, makes them feel heard and understood, and helps them connect with others by letting other people in on their world.

Encouraging people to share things about themselves is a great way to make people like talking with you. This can be done through you leading the conversation but letting them do the talking. If you've ever watched a talk show or listened to a podcast with a guest, you'll notice that the host leads the interaction by asking questions about the other person.

But of course, you're having a conversation and not an interview. There's a fine balance between leading the interaction and encouraging other people to share about themselves, but also sharing about yourself during the process.

One way to get people to talk about themselves is to ask good questions. In order to get on a subject you'd like to talk about, you can directly ask about it or notice it when the subject naturally comes up. From there, you can talk about the surface-level logical details or get into the emotional details.

Asking about the logical details means asking about the what, who, when, where, and how in relation to the topic, which are straightforward and can help get people comfortable talking to you. It can be useful to know certain details, but the real bonding comes when someone gets to talk about—and when you get to understand—their why, their reasoning, and their feelings.

If you and another person are talking about hockey, for example, it's one thing to talk about the latest scores, player stats, and who they think will win the Stanley Cup, but it's another thing to ask about why their favorite team is the Toronto Maple Leafs or how they started watching hockey. Of course, the type of answer you get will depend on how well the other person understands themselves and if they are vulnerable enough to share, but this is a very powerful tool. In a natural flow of a conversation, you'll have both logical and emotional conversation topics, which is a good thing, because both make for a great conversation. Just talking about the logical aspects of life can get pretty boring and dull, while only talking about the emotional side can creep the other person out.

The best way to get people to talk about themselves, however, is to start sharing things about yourself. When you do this, you make the interaction more comfortable for the other person to do the same, instead of coming across as though you're the one doing the asking with no sharing. Share your likes or dislikes, your opinions, your stories, and ask them about theirs. Throughout this book, I've been doing this exact thing. Have you noticed that most of the personal stories I share aren't the ones where everything is awesome and goes right for me but are primarily about the times when I failed or felt bad? These are going to be far more inspiring to you, since I'm making myself relatable. If we were in conversation and I was sharing similar stories, you would likely be much more willing to open up and share your experiences, and more willing to trust and connect with me, because I'm sharing the more important details of my life.

One mistake that many unskilled conversationalists can make is that they keep asking new questions instead of building upon the conversation topic at hand. Asking questions to get the conversation going is just the beginning—from there, you can continue to extend the conversation by asking relevant topics beyond the superficial level and establish further familiarity.

Key Takeaways

- Strong social skills are paramount to your success in being social. The effectiveness of your speech represents how well you can communicate everything going on internally.
- Small talk is important because it allows people to establish a sense of commonality and allows for the people to share and gather information about each other.
- To make your small talk more entertaining, enter conversations with the "yes and . . ." mentality, be knowledgeable about subjects of conversation, be humorous, avoid constantly asking questions, and tell engaging stories.
- You will need to get into deeper conversation to build real connections.
- A good rule of thumb is to transition to deeper connection when you feel comfortable doing so.
- Transitioning to deeper conversations isn't a specific phase or procedure. Rather, it's when you introduce topics of conversation that are more personal and allow you and the person to whom you're speaking to get to know each other better.
- There are a number of miscellaneous social skills you will need to develop, including dealing with awkward silences, keeping a conversation going, ending conversations, group conversations, and nonverbal communication.
- The general principle to being socially intelligent is to try to understand what other people think and how they feel, along with being aware of your influence on other people's thoughts and feelings.

CHAPTER 9

Enjoy Being Alone

There's something fascinating about counterintuitive logic. It's funny because the logic in the way we expect seems to make sense, but the counterintuitive logic makes much more sense.

For example, the less choices you are presented with, the more likely you are to make a happy decision. While a rational mind might think that more options means more possibilities, the correct but counterintuitive logic says that the more choices you have, the more likely you are to be unhappier with your choice, since your mind will naturally wonder how much better off you would've been if you went with any one of the many options. This is the paradox of choice.

The less that you try to change someone's mind, the more likely you are to change someone's mind. Rational logic may tell you to present the other person with more perspectives, more data, and more intense yelling to snap them out of what might be a clearly foolish decision, but this is ineffective. The counterintuitive advice of trying less to convince them takes into consideration the other person's ego. When someone's ego is challenged with the bombardment of arguments, it tends to push against change, but when the person is free to make up their own mind, they are more likely to consider more perspectives, since their ego isn't at risk of being hurt during free thinking.

The more you enjoy being on your own, the more you will enjoy being with others. This too is counterintuitive logic that holds true and will make you more successful socially.

Hold up . . .

What the heck?

This book is supposed to be about making friends and being social. I'm already feeling lonely. Why on earth are you telling me to enjoy being alone?

Even with a rewarding social life, you may spend a good amount of time alone, so we want to make sure you're not using a social life as an escape for dealing with issues that you may be avoiding. Plus, being comfortable with being alone will make you far less needy in your social relationships.

How you design your own life is going to greatly affect how rich your social life can be. If your personal life consists of doing interesting things, trying new things, and having new adventures, your social life will become much better as a result. Not only will you have a more fulfilling life in general, but you will have new and interesting things to talk about, and the activities you engage in can be avenues towards meeting new people.

However, *being alone should not be the main focus for your social life.* Being around people you care about is the only sustainable, long-term strategy.

Home Alone

What do you like to do when you're home alone? Perhaps you already have a few things you enjoy doing that make you really happy. If you have those things, do them, but from now on, do them unapologetically. Do you lose track of time playing video games? Does writing and thinking deeply about a subject make you happy like it does for me? Does finding new recipes for food make you feel joyful inside? If you have a thing you really like, enjoy it freely.

Sometimes we suppress our passions because we may not think they're a productive use of our time, or we think we "should" be doing something different. There is a time and place to do productive things, but ultimately doing what makes you happy is what counts—so do it.

If you don't currently have passions you love, this is a great opportunity to try new things. New passions can fall under one of three broad categories: consuming, learning, or creating. Although learning and creating can be more productive and "beneficial" than consuming, don't feel pressured to stick to these categories if you prefer to consume. The most important thing is that you try new things, without judgement. Don't knock it until you try it.

CONSUMING

Consuming is when you acquire and/or enjoy a product or service. This is the easiest and usually most relaxing form of a hobby because these activities are usually passive or only slightly engaging.

Consuming is a great way to relax and enjoy yourself, but it can be easy to get into the trap of overconsuming to a point where productivity in other areas of your life may drop. Playing too many video games, watching too much Netflix, and excessive scrolling on your phone can affect your social life, work, or bigger life goals, so definitely be mindful of these habits.

The truth is that lots of forms of consumption are designed to be addictive, since the companies making the products or services have to compete more and more for your attention and money, so beware of this.

Things you can consume include:

- Video games
- Movies and shows
- Sports
- YouTube and internet videos
- Blogs and books
- Food and drink
- Music

LEARNING

Learning is similar to consuming, but it has a distinct purpose. Learning is a great thing to be passionate about because your brain naturally craves learning new information. Learning new things had a direct impact on our survival as a species, which can explain the amazing rush of joy you can get if you learn something new. This can be a great source of fulfillment when you're alone.

If you're on your own, the mediums you can learn from boil down to a few: books, internet articles and blogs, online videos, online courses, podcasts, and scientific literature.

While the mediums may be a select few, the topics you can learn about are virtually endless. Here are only some of the topics you can learn about:

- Self-improvement
- Mindset
  - Productivity
  - Social skills
  - Dating and relationships
- Health and fitness
- Sports
- History
- Business
- Money and investing
- Science
- Art
- Food and drink
- Politics
- Music
- Automobiles and machinery
- Animals and wildlife

CREATING

The last big category that hobbies at home can fall under is creating. Creating is a powerful hobby, not only because it takes skill to build something of value that you or other people can benefit from, but also because it can put you into a serious state of flow.

In psychology, a flow state is when you're fully immersed in an activity and you have energized focus, complete involvement, and are enjoying the process of the activity. When you're in a flow state, you're connected to the idea or activity you're doing, which can help you avoid loneliness when alone.

Covid-19 Creating Time

In 2020, Covid-19 was starting to enter Canada, the country I live in. Our country progressively went into lockdown. This meant that the rest of my school semester was going to be online. Final exams were pretty much all canceled, my summer job was going to be canceled, and I would be living on my own for the foreseeable future since I couldn't go back to my hometown to be with my family. You could probably guess the dread I had knowing this lockdown could last many months.

I had no job, pretty much no school, and no friends to see. How was I supposed to keep myself from going insane? I found a hobby: creating. I've always been fascinated by creating a business because I wanted to make money solving real problems, and my stints doing sales for successful startups only fueled my desire. Now that I will have at least five months of solitude with no job to keep me busy, I might as well do it now.

I didn't end up creating a business, but I started a private blog series on how to develop the confidence to approach women in real life. The problem I identified was that meeting women was hard for me, and it probably was hard for many other men too. Online apps were pretty ineffective (although it's a great concept), using social circles was good although the quantity of women could be low, so I figured that going up and approaching women was the only real way to find what I was looking for.

Developing the confidence to approach women isn't so much about what to say or how to act; it's more of a self-improvement process to transform yourself into a person that women want by developing the traits and proofs they desire. Most of the focus of my writing was on things like physical and mental health, reprogramming mindsets and beliefs, vulnerability, overcoming insecurities, being respectable, dressing well, building a lifestyle that makes you happy, social skills, and social intelligence—sound familiar? After completing it, I made the decision to hold the project for the time being.

After completing the project, I still had another big problem: I was in lockdown for quite a few more months, so what did I do? Naturally, I went back to asking myself about the problems I could solve, and I discovered through my last failed venture that I really like writing. I wasn't exactly going to let my last few months of intensive hard work go to waste, and from there, I discovered a related problem that I also had—developing a social life.

Because I found a new hobby that I loved doing, I've been quite happy, focused, and productive for what could have otherwise been a miserable, lonely time.

Unlike consumption, creating is a hobby that can impact your life in more ways than just experiencing immediate joy. It's similar to learning, in a sense, but the benefits are more direct. I had to apply my learning to something to make it valuable for others. And my hobby of creating is directly beneficial for you, as you are reading this book right now.

Some categories within creating include:

- Book
- Blog
- Business
- Website

- Photography
- Videography
- Computer coding
- Digital design
- Visual arts
- Music
- Dance
- Cooking/baking
- Woodwork
- Automobiles and machinery
- Gardening
- Sewing/knitting
- Scrapbooking

Go Do Cool Things

Just because you don't have a friend to accompany you, it doesn't mean you have to isolate yourself inside your house all the time. You can definitely do lots of cool, interesting things outside the house.

Spending many hours or even days on end inside can have some negative consequences. For one, your mental health can become distorted, as you're not as in touch with reality and other people—instead, you're being exposed to screens for long periods of time.

A good way to find out what you like to do outside the house is to ask yourself this: If you had to spend an entire day outside the house, what would you do?

There are likely many things you want to do but haven't yet done. The best time to try those things is now.

Fear of uncertainty is what stops most people from trying new things, not time or money. Their lives are predictable. Anything that brings uncertainty is to be avoided—this is human nature. But human nature doesn't really bode well for helping you have some fun in your life.

When I realized that life is all about not knowing and doing something anyway, I started to supercharge my lifestyle by trying new things.

If you want to try boxing, you're not going to know exactly what to expect when you walk into the gym on the first day of class. You probably won't know what's going on, or how to throw a proper punch, and you may be quite nervous, but that's the whole point—to not know and do something anyway.

To help you get started, try this exercise. Create a bucket list of everything you want to try. Don't filter yourself here. Just write, write, write whatever comes to your mind.

For each item, ask yourself: How can I try it once? Keep in mind financial costs or time required, but remember that it's worth trying things you have a desire to try, at least once. It's about finding the courage and creativity to do so. This also goes without saying, but use some common sense here too. If you put playing football with crocodiles or skydiving without a parachute on your list, hopefully you're smart enough to figure out what is a rational idea and what isn't.

After you make the list, take the route that requires the least financial cost or time. When we want to take on a new hobby, we think we need to spend a lot of money on it or spend a lot of time doing so. That doesn't have to be the case. When first starting out, try your new hobby once and figure out how to do it for free or at a low cost, so you can try many different things without overcommitting.

The weird, strange, odd, but pretty cool things you think of are up to you, but here is a list of more common things you can try:

- Activities
    - Weightlifting, biking, running, martial arts, swimming, sports, golf, bowling, airsoft, pool/billiards, video games, chess or board games, thrifting, skateboarding, poker or cards, fishing, hunting, archery, canoeing, hiking, camping, skiing or snowboarding
- Community
    - Coaching, volunteering, teaching, fundraising or doing charity, visiting an animal shelter

Terrible Things to Do When You're Lonely

When you're alone, you may end up also feeling lonely. Although those two feelings are linked, they are not the same thing. Being alone is something we all experience, whether it's spending a weekend in, having no friends to meet up with, or because we just moved to a new city and don't know anyone. But being lonely is different. Being lonely is the feeling of lacking connection with something, whether it's a person, yourself, an activity, the world, or an idea.

The simple trick to not feel lonely in the moment is to connect yourself to something. If it's not a person, is it an activity?

Can you get into a state of flow learning or creating something? Can you find something new you want to consume?

Of course, there are going to be moments when you don't feel connected to anything, and this is where mindfulness comes in. Staying in the present moment, instead of thinking about what you did in the past, what you're missing out on, or what you want to happen, will help you stay grounded.

Limit the primary culprits that are making you feel lonely. Many of these culprits take you out of the present moment and drag your thoughts into other places that inevitably make you feel lonely.

ENDLESSLY SCROLL SOCIAL MEDIA

When you are feeling lonely, what's the thing you tend to do more? Pick up the phone and browse social media. This isn't an accident. Aside from the entertainment factor, using social media more when you're alone is by design. Social media is designed for you to get a sense of "connection" with others as you are exposed to people or their profiles.

The problem comes when we get exposed to people's highlight reels of life during the moments we feel the worst. It's hard not to feel bad about yourself when you are feeling lonely and then see three friends posting about a party, a few people posting about restaurants or bars they're at, and a couple posting cute, loving photos.

It can be hard to break away from your social-media use, which is why if you want to limit social-media use, you should focus on getting yourself in a state of flow with an activity.

USE NEGATIVE WORDS

What words do you use when you're alone? Words have a significant impact on our thoughts because they're what our minds use to interpret the world. When you use words, you are sending information to your brain about what you're interpreting, so what words are you using?

Are you using words such as *lonely*, *loser*, *stupid*, *no one*, *no life*, *lame*, *dumb*, *unlikeable*, *loner*, and *hate* to describe you and your situation when you feel alone, or are you using words like *love*, *like*, *cool*, *interesting*, *great*, and *smart*?

I knew I was becoming satisfied with spending time alone when I stopped calling myself a lonely loser. Every time I would spend a Friday night alone, a weekend alone, or see people on social media posting with their friends, I'd instantly call myself a lonely loser, which would throw off my mood for a while. Now when I spend a Friday night alone, a weekend alone, or see people on social media posting with their friends, I don't even come close to calling myself anything remotely negative. If there's a problem, I'll fix it, but there's a lot to enjoy being alone, too.

If you use negative words, it's obvious why you feel bad when you're alone. The information you're sending to your brain is pessimistic. The way to make the shift is to work on staying present. When you're present, you can witness your thoughts pass without judgement, and from there, you can consciously shift toward using positive words.

HAVE A NEGATIVE OUTLOOK

What do you think about the future—in this case, your social life? Do you tend to think being alone is forever and you're destined for a life of doom and gloom, or do you tend to think that your situation can change and be better?

Your outlook is important because it changes how your brain thinks and how creative it gets. If you think that your future is going to be hopeless, your brain doesn't do much creative thinking because you're telling it that the future is going to be negative—why would it put effort into thinking? Conversely, if you have an optimistic view on your future, your brain tends to become creative because it needs to think about ways to stay in line with your optimistic thoughts.

When I first recognized that spending time alone was a problem, I beat myself up for it. I used to call myself a loner and a loser, and I used to think this was the way it was going to be forever. But now when I spend time alone, I recognize that I'm going to spend time alone and it's okay, I'm neither a loner nor a loser, I have quite a good perception of myself, and I look forward to the next time I get to see a friend. Of course, this comes with improving your current situation, which is the point of this book, but also it comes with having a healthier relationship with spending time alone.

Once again, being alone shouldn't be a dominant, long-term strategy because humans are designed to be social and not isolated for long periods of time. Being connected to ideas and activities, staying present, and spending time alone without feeling lonely are all good solutions to the short-term effects of feeling lonely, but nothing can replace actual human interaction. Without human connection, many of these ideas and activities can start to feel pointless and meaningless, which is why this is only a short-term strategy or a band-aid solution to a bigger problem.

Key Takeaways

- Even with a rewarding social life, you may spend a good amount of time alone.
- Coping with loneliness by enjoying being alone should not be the main focus for your social life. Being around people you care about is the only sustainable long-term strategy.
- When you're at home, you can do what you like or find something to do that you like. This can come in the form of consuming, learning, or creating.
- When you're outside your home, it's worth finding activities you like. This can create opportunities to meet new people.
- When you're feeling lonely, you shouldn't excessively browse social media, use negative words to interpret your situation, or have a negative outlook.

Live Outside the Box to Box

After reading this book, you should have a good sense of what it takes to live outside the box to box. Not only does this book provide you with the blueprint to creating a rewarding social life with strong connections with those you like, but also it provides you ways to improve yourself to become a person who can create that social life.

But at the end of the day, this is all theory.

Theory isn't going to be the thing that brings you friendship, makes you confident, or makes you socially skilled—taking action is. Theory is just giving you the map, but you still have to walk the path. However, this should be one of, if not the most worthwhile journeys you ever take. Nothing in life is more important than the people you choose to surround yourself with. The money, status, prestige, and luxury goods are nice to have, but the relationships are crucial.

As your author, I have nothing else to say other than: go out and experience it! Take action, make mistakes, be vulnerable, laugh it off, and enjoy the good times. If you manage to accomplish that, I would have done my job.

If this book helped you, I'd love to know. Please send me an email at tak@rocketshippublishing.com to connect.

As a thank you for finishing this book, I'd like to offer you a free guide that will help you take action and get results in any of the skills or traits you would like to develop. This guide should make creating your rewarding social life much easier.

If you'd like this gift, simply go to https://rocketshippublishing.com/free-gift or email me.

If I could ask a favor from you before we go, *could you be so kind as to leave a review of this book and share it with your network?* This would be the best way to spread the message, and I would be eternally grateful.

If at any point, you feel like you need my personal help in taking action and improving your social life, please visit https://rocketshippublishing.com/consulting or email me.

That's all I have for you. I hope you enjoyed reading this book as much as I have enjoyed writing it for you.

Best of luck in your journey,

Tak Maeda
Author at Rocketship Publishing

References

"Cigna Takes Action to Combat the Rise of Loneliness and Improve Mental Wellness in America," January 23, 2020. Cigna. https://www.cigna.com/about-us/newsroom/news-and-views/press-releases/2020/cigna-takes-action-to-combat-the-rise-of-loneliness-and-improve-mental-wellness-in-america.

Fung, Jason. "My Single Best Tip for a Healthy Weight: Online Fasting Method for Intermittent Fasting." The Fasting Method, August 17, 2020. https://thefastingmethod.com/my-single-best-tip-for-a-healthy-weight/.

Hall, Jeffrey A. "How Many Hours Does It Take to Make a Friend?" Journal of Social and Personal Relationships 36, no. 4 (2018): 1278–96. https://doi.org/10.1177/0265407518761225.

Mineo, Liz. "Over Nearly 80 Years, Harvard Study Has Been Showing How to Live a Healthy and Happy Life." Harvard Gazette. Harvard Gazette, November 26, 2018. https://news.harvard.edu/gazette/story/2017/04/over-nearly-80-years-harvard-study-has-been-showing-how-to-live-a-healthy-and-happy-life/.

Snell, K. D. "The Rise of Living Alone and Loneliness in History." Social History 42, no. 1 (2017): 2–28. https://doi.org/10.1080/03071022.2017.1256093.

Made in the USA
Monee, IL
01 August 2021

74723708R00135